To Augusta,

Love and Peace.

Gena Olsson

Remembering Forever

a journey
of darkness
and light

Dr. Eva Olsson

Holocaust Survivor and Author of UNLOCKING THE DOORS

with Ron Jacques

Copyright © 2008 by Eva Olsson

Cover Photo: Ron Jacques

Trip Photographs Copyright © 2007 by Ron Jacques

Cover and Page Layout Design: Kari O'Neill

Printed in Canada by Rose Printing

ISBN 978-0-9810671-0-0

Library of Congress Cataloging

10 9 8 7 6 5 4 3 2

Published by Eva Olsson

Bracebridge Ontario

In memory of the millions of people whose
voices have been silenced by the forces of hate.

In the hope that you will never be forgotten.

Acknowledgements

Ioan (Johnny) Popescu, Rob and Lia Larcombe, and Olimpia and Georghe Iancu, who helped make our visit to Sighet, Romania, one of the highlights of the trip.

Yvonne and Don Gray, who were good company on a difficult journey;

Linda Ann Jewell, who helped with some of the travel arrangements;

Jan Olsson, my son, for his encouragement and support for this journey;

Kari O'Neill (www.whitespacecreative.ca), and Brent Trinier (www.roseprinting.ca), for their expertise and willingness to go way beyond "just business" in the design and printing of this book;

Don Smith, Dan Wyjad and his secretary, Jennifer Garrow-Sneyd, for ongoing support;

Bill Van Wyck, who tweaked the cover picture and designed the map of the journey.

Thanks to those people who gave financial support to this project.

CONTENTS

Introduction

Chapter One   **Before the Journey**   1

Chapter Two   **Budapest**   7

Chapter Three   **Satu Mare**   25

Chapter Four   **Sighet**   41

Chapter Five   **Auschwitz-Birkenau**   65

Chapter Six   **Buchenwald**   99

Chapter Seven   **Bergen-Belsen**   129

Chapter Eight   **Sweden**   145

Chapter Nine   **After the Journey**   181

Epilogue   205

INTRODUCTION

Fear not your enemies, for they can only kill you.

Fear not your friends, for they can only betray you.

Fear only the indifferent, who permit the killers

and betrayers to walk safely on the earth.

*Edward Yashinsky, Yiddish poet
from Poland, who survived
the Holocaust only to die in a
Communist prison in Poland*

On September 18, 2007, Eva and I flew out of Toronto, starting a 28-day journey to retrace her life. During that time, we visited five countries—Hungary, Romania, Poland, Germany, and Sweden—travelling primarily by train. For all of the trip except Sweden, we were accompanied by Don Gray and his wife, Yvonne. Don was making a documentary film about Eva—*Stronger Than Fire: The Eva Olsson Story.*

While we were travelling, and in the eight months since our return on October 15, 2007, Eva and I have been sitting down and talking about the trip, recording our conversations as we did so. Sometimes we would look at pictures from the trip to stimulate our memories, and sometimes I would ask questions to expand on or clarify Eva's thoughts. Once these conversations had been transcribed, I began the editing process as well as trying to pair content with photographs from the trip.

While the basic organization of the book follows the chronology of the trip, I tried to place the discussion of certain themes where I felt they worked best, even if they could apply to more than one place in the book. In addition to this material, at times I went back to the first book Eva and I had worked on together, her autobiography *Unlocking the Doors: A Woman's Struggle Against Intolerance*, and copied or adapted material that would give context to aspects of the trip without having to go through it all again with Eva. I wanted this book to be able to stand alone, making sense even if the reader hadn't read the first book.

The trip was an emotional roller coaster, with visits to concentration camps interspersed with relaxing/gruelling train trips, meeting interesting people, enjoying the ever-changing regional cuisine. Memories of the trip continue to reverberate for both of us, and we find our thoughts and responses changing as time passes. I expect that will continue to happen.

The Holocaust is in the process of evolving from a collection of memories into history. It won't be long before there are no more survivors and first-hand witnesses to tell their stories. If this transformation into history is not handled carefully, we may experience a revival of this kind of evil in the future. Professor Yehuda Bauer, director of the International Center for Holocaust Studies at the Institute of Contemporary Jewry, Israel, expressed it this way: "Because it happened once, it can happen again, not in the same form, not necessarily to the same people, not by the same people, but to anyone by anyone. It was unprecedented, but now the precedent is there."

Some of the pictures that we see in the newspapers and on television—Rwanda, Darfur, Bosnia, Congo, Cambodia—are frighteningly similar to the images of the Holocaust. In many of these cases people are being starved and slaughtered because of their ethnicity, or for the mere fact of their existence. It seems that no matter how often we tell ourselves, "Never again," there is a regime somewhere in the world willing to prove us wrong.

As we surveyed the horrors at each concentration camp, the thought crossed my mind that it was almost as if there had been a competition to see which camp could devise the most horrific ways to torture and humiliate Jews before killing them. Looking at the displays in the camps, Eva said to me several times, "I know they wanted to kill us, but why all this?" That question stayed with me and haunted me as I began to work on this book. Who could hate a group of people so much that they would do such things to them? Were the perpetrators just a tiny minority of the population who were out of control, unbeknownst to the rest of the population? Or did Hitler tap into a much larger pool of anti-Semitism, realizing as he proceeded that very few people or countries were going to come to the defence of the Jews?

Anti-Semitism has been a fact of life in many countries in the world for centuries, but why had no country ever set out to do what Germany tried to do—annihilate an entire group of people, all the Jews of Europe? This question is still very controversial, and there is disagreement among historians as to how much the German population knew about what their government and armies were doing in their name. In his book *Hitler's Willing Executioners: Ordinary Germans and the Holocaust*, Daniel Goldhagen makes the case that "ordinary Germans, nurtured in a society where Jews were seen as unalterably evil and dangerous, willingly followed their beliefs to their logical conclusion. ... [T]he extermination of European Jewry engaged the energies and enthusiasm of tens of thousands of ordinary Germans." Other historians disagree with Goldhagen and point to different reasons why Hitler was able to get away with what he did. Regardless, all acknowledge that Hitler made anti-Semitism a basic tenet of his National Socialism doctrine. When his Nazi Party gained power, they began to take steps to implement the "Final Solution to the Jewish Question"— extermination.

At many times during the war, even at the very end when Germany could see that it was not going to win, the extermination of Jews continued at a furious pace. Trains and troops that were needed in the war effort were used instead to facilitate the extermination of as many Jews as possible. Historians have noted that for some Nazis, elimination of the Jews appears to have been a higher priority than winning the war.

When Eva was talking to a woman in Satu Mare, Romania and mentioned the Holocaust, the woman said, "Oh well, it was war." Another woman (in Canada) told her that it was "time to move on and get over it." Interestingly, this type of comment is markedly different from those we heard from young people we talked to on the trip. Young Germans all said that they feel the weight of their country's history and are resigned to the fact that it will always be with them. Several expressed the worry that things were heading in that direction again.

At the 2005 ceremony marking the 60th anniversary of the liberation of Bergen-Belsen, Christian Wulff, the Prime Minister of Lower Saxony, expressed a similar viewpoint:

How do we Germans of the following generations deal with the burden of our past—a burden [that] cannot and must not be allowed to fade into oblivion? ...Young people in particular find it difficult; that could not be otherwise. We try to absorb our knowledge of the events that took place here; research findings over the decades have supplied us with increasingly precise facts and revealed the overall connections—and yet we still cannot grasp what happened. But these shameful memories are the source of our responsibility for the present and for the future...That defamation, segregation, and the gradual deprivation of the rights of minority groups were the first step towards the ultimate catastrophe. ...That is why we have to appeal to people's minds, not just here at this memorial site, but everywhere, especially at our schools. We have to refute comparisons that are intended to play down the horror of what happened. We have to combat right-wing extremism and antisemitism at an early stage...It is our joint responsibility across the generations, whether in our memories or looking to the future, to remain on constant vigil, to be alert to any form whatsoever of extremism and totalitarianism, to any form of intolerance and xenophobia. These terrible events must never be allowed to happen again...We owe it to our children and our children's children that they, too, learn to commemorate the victims, to ensure that they are willing to recognize dangers at an early stage and take timely action against these dangers—dangers which threaten human rights and our democratic constitution.

At the same ceremony, Sam Bloch, President of the World Federation of Bergen-Belsen Associations, said:

Our commemoration should help people everywhere better understand the warning bells of unconstrained racial and religious hatred and bigotry that are sounding globally unchallenged in our times now. Today, on this occasion of the 60th anniversary of the liberation, some people say to us that it is time to forget; it is time to heal old wounds. We reject such statements, which are not only historically false, but an insult to the memory of our martyrs, and a danger of history repeating itself in a world of turmoil and strife, hatred and terrorism.

Former Swedish Prime Minister Göran Persson, speaking at a Holocaust conference in Stockholm in 2000, put it this way:

It is the end of the silence, and the beginning of a new millennium.

The Holocaust will always hold universal meaning. Although we have left the century in which the Holocaust occurred, we

must continue to study it in all its dimensions, at all times. We must add more pieces to the puzzle, foster greater awareness of the causes, acquire more knowledge about the consequences.

But if we think that more research about the Holocaust will provide us with answers that are crystal clear, then we are mistaken. If we think that more education will mean clear-cut, ready-made solutions that each of us can grasp, then we are mistaken.

Some of the answers will always be beyond our grasp. But that must never ever lead us to the conclusion that it is pointless to seek them!

It is the only way to prevent a future where people have the answers engraved on their skin.

We will never forget; it must never happen again.

Ron Jacques
June 2008

Stoc

Sw

▲ Trellel

▲ Lübeck

Bergen-Belsen
✛

● Berlin

▲ Hannover

Buchenwald ✛
▲ Weimar

Germany

Czech

France

Austri

Italy

MAP OF JOURNEY

1

BEFORE THE JOURNEY

Why would I want to revisit hell? It took courage
to go back into the darkness, but I found light
there too.

Eva Olsson

When people heard that I was taking a journey to retrace my life, the first question they asked was, "Why do you want to go back?" When I turned 75 I was asked to replace another Holocaust survivor and go to the concentration camps with March for the Living, an annual event started in 1988, where people walk the three kilometres between Auschwitz I and Auschwitz II (Birkenau) in memory of those who died there. At that time I said, "No way. I'm not going at this age." I asked myself why I would want to set foot in the place where I was born, where I used to have dozens of relatives, knowing there would be no one waiting for me. Why would I want to revisit the hell of the concentration camps where my family and I had been imprisoned?

Later, when I was writing my autobiography, *Unlocking the Doors*, I did want to go back and search my roots, but at that time I couldn't afford to go. But here I was in 2007, 82 years of age, finally taking that journey, hoping I would come away from the trip with knowledge I didn't have before, knowledge that might bring me peace, and perhaps some closure too.

One reason I didn't ever want to go back was my fear that some of the people who had committed genocide there might still be around. I had also heard from friends that there was still a lot of anti-Semitism there. When I lived in Europe, I had a difficult time with fear, and I brought that fear with me across the ocean to Canada. I have been dealing with those feelings over the years, and going back on this trip was a step in the right direction. I wanted to conquer those fears and get rid of some of that huge emotional load.

I wanted to go to Satu Mare, my hometown in Romania, because that's where I had grown up. The Nazis had deported us from there suddenly on May 15, 1944, and I wanted to go back and walk the streets I had known as a child.

I wanted to go to Auschwitz-Birkenau because so many members of my family died there in 1944—my mom, my sister, my brother, five nieces, my grandparents. I wanted to place a candle on the train tracks inside the camp so they would know they would never be forgotten.

I wanted to go to Buchenwald, where my father died of starvation at the age of 48. My father and I had a difficult relationship, and I wanted to see if I could find some peace, some closure. I have no idea where his bones or ashes are, but I wanted to walk on the same ground he last walked on.

I wanted to go to Bergen-Belsen because that's where I was finally liberated from the Nazi killing machine. I wanted to pay my respects and say thank you to those soldiers who gave their lives to free us.

I wanted to end the trip in Sweden because that's the country that accepted me as a refugee and helped me get settled with a job and a place to live. I wanted to revisit the places that were special to me and my late husband Rude when we lived there prior to coming to Canada. I wanted to reconnect with

Rude's family, as we had lost contact over the years. I had some unfinished things to do there as well, and I hoped to find closure too.

The most painful thing was not having my husband Rude with me. We came to Canada in 1951 because I was afraid of another war in Europe. Rude was injured in a car accident and died in 1964. For many years after his death I felt very bad and wondered if he would still be alive if only we hadn't left Sweden. But I have learned to accept the fact that "if only" doesn't change anything.

I want to share this journey with others, to show them what hate has done in the past and is capable of doing in the future if we don't pay attention to the warning signs. I hope that the younger generations following us can learn from my experiences and do what is necessary to stop it from happening again.

Those are some of the reasons why I needed to make this journey. I knew it wouldn't be easy, but that was okay, because I am a survivor who has dealt with more difficult things in my life. All my life I have dealt with problems by facing them, taking one step at a time. It took courage to go back into the darkness, but I found light there too.

Before the Journey

2

BUDAPEST

Budapest is a beautiful city, but it was full of sad memories for me.

Eva Olsson

At the turn of the 20th century, one out of every three citizens in Budapest was Jewish. Before World War II, approximately 200,000 Jews lived in Budapest. When the war began, Hungary allied itself with Nazi Germany, but in March 1944, Germany occupied Hungary. Between April and July 1944, the Nazis, with the active help of Hungarian clerks, policemen, and soldiers deported 437,000 people—more than fifty percent of all the Jews in Hungary—from the provinces outside Budapest. In fact, by the end of July, the Jews in Budapest were virtually the only Jews remaining in Hungary.

In October 1944, Germany instigated a coup and a new Hungarian government dominated by the fascist Arrow Cross party took power. When Jews began to look for places to hide, Swedish diplomat Raoul Wallenberg and other foreign diplomats organized false papers and safe houses for them. They are credited with saving thousands of Jews.

In November 1944, the Arrow Cross ordered the remaining Jews in Budapest into a closed ghetto. Between December 1944 and the end of January 1945, the Arrow Cross took as many as 20,000 Jews from the ghetto to the banks of the Danube, shot them, and threw their bodies into the river.

When Soviet forces liberated Budapest on February 13, 1945, more than 100,000 Jews remained in the city. The Nazis and their European accomplices murdered six million Jews during World War II. Out of a total of 825,000 Hungarian Jews, 550,000 died—nearly one tenth of the total number of Holocaust victims.

Eva and I arrived in Budapest on September 19, 2007, a bit jet-lagged after our flight from Toronto via Frankfurt. Don and Yvonne were scheduled to arrive in the late afternoon on September 20, so Eva and I had some time to look around the city. We took a bus tour of the main attractions of both Pest, where we were staying, and Buda, which sits on a hill across the Danube River.

The main thing Eva wanted to do while we were in Budapest was visit her oldest sister Sarah's grave. Sarah had died in a hospital in Buda in January 1944. One problem was that there are two Jewish cemeteries, one in Buda and one in Pest, and Eva didn't know which one Sarah was buried in.

As we were walking back to our hotel, we saw signs pointing to the synagogue, so we went down that street. I noticed that the young security guard at the gate was moved as he talked to Eva, and at one point he reached out and held her hand. A woman at the synagogue called one of the cemeteries, but they said they needed Sarah's married name in order to find the records showing where she was buried. Eva didn't know Sarah's married name, so we couldn't find out where she was buried. We didn't get this information until we were at the archives in her hometown, Satu Mare, several days later.

We needed to get back to the hotel to meet Don and Yvonne, so we limited our visit that day to the museum at the synagogue. There was a display of pictures of Auschwitz-Birkenau concentration camp in one corner of the museum. I hadn't expected this, and I looked over at Eva to see how she was reacting. Eva looked at them in silence. I realized that the display was a foreshadowing of what lay ahead of us on this trip. When we went back the next day, the synagogue was closed because of Yom Kippur, the New Year. Eva recalled that before she had left Bracebridge to start the trip, a man had said to her: "What a way to start the New Year." In more ways than one.

On September 21, as Don was filming, we walked around the area that had been the Jewish ghetto during WWII. At one point we found a plaque commemorating January 16, 1945, the day the Soviets tore down the ghetto wall. Behind the synagogue we saw the Holocaust Heroes memorial—a silver weeping willow sculpture, a symbol of mourning whose leaves have the names of murdered Jews engraved on them. Initially, we thought the willow might be a Jewish tradition, but as we traveled in Hungary and Romania, we saw many weeping willow symbols on Christian gravestones as well.

Throughout our travels in Hungary and Romania, but in Sweden as well, doors and gates into Jewish buildings, cemeteries, and stores were locked, and we had to be buzzed

in by the security people inside. Either that, or there was a security guard standing at the entrance who checked us over before allowing us to enter. Whenever we asked about this, we were told that it was to prevent attacks on the premises, an ever-present threat in Europe even today. At one point we asked a woman at the (locked) Judean shop where we could find information about the Jewish cemeteries, and she directed us to a building just around the corner. The large wooden door to this building wasn't locked, so we pushed it open and went inside. A security guard who was talking to some people in a courtyard beyond the entrance came running over to us and demanded to see what Don had filmed. Even as we were explaining how we had got there and what we wanted, he was threatening to call the police unless he could see the film footage. Eventually Eva went with him to his office, gave him information about us, and we left. After he had calmed down a bit, the guard told us that the cemetery would also be closed for Yom Kippur.

Eva and I had lunch at Central, a large bistro near the Danube, stopped in a church to hear an organist and singer practicing, then rode the Metro and a tram back to the hotel. It was a very pleasant way to spend an afternoon in a beautiful city, a calm before the storm that was to come when we moved on two days later. Young Hungarians always stood and offered Eva their seats on the Metro and buses—with a smile—very impressive.

After checking in at our hotel in Pest, we decided to go for a

walk, and just down the block from our hotel, we were passing a bakery when Eva spotted Dobos torte, her favourite cake. That took Eva back to her childhood:

When I saw that bake shop, and the Dobos torte, I had to have a piece. It took me back to when I was a young child in Satu Mare, my home town, when my uncle Wolf, my mother's older brother, used to visit. He would give me some pennies and I would run to the bake shop and buy a slice of Dobos torte, because that was my favourite. It's made out of about six layers of yellow cake with a butter-cocoa filling, with hazelnuts, and a caramel topping. You have to have a hot knife to slice it. I have the recipe in my Hungarian cookbook. I have made it once; maybe I should make it again.

Budapest is a beautiful city, but it was full of sad memories for me. One thing I really wanted to do was visit my oldest sister Sarah's grave because I was there when she died.

Sarah had become very ill in the fall of 1943, and for months the doctors in Satu Mare were unable to diagnose her illness. In January 1944, my father and I took her by ambulance to a hospital in Budapest, a six-hour drive, while my mother stayed at home with Sarah's three children, aged one to three.

Sarah had not been happy in her arranged marriage to a tall, thin, red-bearded Hasidic man. I felt sorry for Sarah because she was always pregnant; she had three children in four years. When she complained to our mom that her husband spent all his time in the synagogue while she baked bread and cakes for wealthy neighbours, my father gave her husband pep talks about helping his wife more often. But they had no effect, so sometimes I helped her with the heavy loads. When we took Sarah to the hospital in Budapest, her husband was in hiding from the army or the Germans—I never knew why—and no one knew where he was.

My father and I stayed in a room he rented from a family on a side street in the old Jewish section of Pest. I remember that we walked out to a square, took a bus down Rakoczi Street, and crossed the Danube to visit Sarah in the hospital in Buda. As we walked along the streets this time I knew we were in the right area, but I couldn't remember which house we had stayed in.

I would sit by Sarah's bed and my father would stand at the foot of the bed. Most of the time she was out of it; her eyes were hazy. One day Sarah commented on how beautiful the outfit was that I was wearing. My mother had made me a blue jumper dress—no sleeves—out of a wool material. It had an overlap, two rows of buttons like a double-breasted suit. Underneath it I wore a yellow long-sleeved blouse.

When I think back now to that time in Budapest, I can still see my father praying and pacing the floor, crying and offering his life if God would spare Sarah. I realize now that God did spare her—from going to the gas chamber with her children. She died peacefully in a bed in a large, bright hospital room, with my father and me at her side, and she had a proper burial. That was more than the rest of her family got. Four months later, we were in a boxcar being taken to Auschwitz-Birkenau. My mom was crying and hugging Sarah's children. When I asked her why she was crying, she said she was crying for her children, not crying for herself. "I have lived," she said. She was 49. She also said how she envied Sarah because Sarah had a proper burial. That statement haunted me for a very long time. Why would she say that? Did she have a feeling? Did she know that something bad was going to happen to her family? Probably.

I knew Sarah's struggle was over when they called a *minyan*—10 Jewish men who had to be present for certain prayers—to give her the last rites. On January 11, 1944, after ten days in the hospital, Sarah died of encephalitis, leaving three little girls and no father around to take care of them. Some women washed her body and put her in a white gown, and that's the last time I saw her. I wish now I had known Sarah better.

My dad could not tell my mother Sarah had died, so he sent her a telegram saying that we were coming home and would have to leave my sister in the sanatorium. Following Jewish tradition, Sarah was buried that same day in Budapest. We cried on the train ride back to Satu Mare, wondering how we were going to face her children. I can still see my mother's face when we got home. She was crying terribly; she knew Sarah had died. We mourned Sarah's death in the traditional Jewish way by sitting on the floor for seven days (*shiva*). We covered the mirrors, dipped hard-boiled eggs in ashes and ate them, and made cuts on our coat lapels.

On this latest visit to Budapest, we went to a nearby restaurant, the Huszar, for dinner. Two musicians were playing, a violinist and an accordionist, and we enjoyed the music so much we made a reservation to return the following evening. One of the Hungarian songs I asked the musicians to play was about Satu Mare, my hometown. It reminded me of the orange trees blossoming—little white flowers with orange inside—along the Szamos River. As a child of 11 or 12, I used to walk along the river and look at the people in the cafes that used to be there. I realize now that it was a way for me to get away from the restrictions of my home and see another way of living.

Another song was about a man asking a bird to take a letter to his mother, asking her to forget about him and not to cry. I often sing those songs when I'm driving along country roads on long trips. It was very emotional for me to hear those songs again.

I have no desire to go back to Budapest because I didn't come away with positive feelings. My only connection with that city is that my sister is buried there. I felt like an outsider there, and the people weren't particularly warm to us. I didn't know much about what happened to the Jews in Budapest until later. What the Arrow Cross did wasn't much different than what the Nazis did. They killed people and sent their clothes and shoes away to Germany.

Sadly, I am hearing from people that there is still a lot of antisemitism in Hungary, Romania, and other countries in Europe. Recently, a friend was admiring an airport in Austria and an Austrian man said to her: "Yes, we have Herr Hitler to thank for this."

The shoes sit on the concrete embankment along the Pest side of the Duna (Danube) River. Most sit facing the river, looking as if their owners had recently stepped out of them and walked away. Some of the shoes lay on their sides, others stood side-by-side; some were everyday plain and others were dress-up fancy. A pair of women's boots lay beside a small child's pair of shoes, next to a single work boot, alongside high heels. Strollers coming upon them in the bright sunlight react in a variety of ways. Some examine the shoes with interest, pointing out a particular pair to companions, ooh-ing and aww-ing over a pair of buttoned-up women's high boots or a tiny pair of children's shoes. Others place their feet beside a pair of shoes, pretending they are trying them on, and posing for pictures, all smiles and giggles.

But other strollers' faces are unsmiling and drawn as they walk slowly beside the shoes, some stopping to wipe tears from their cheeks, others standing quietly, shoulders shaking slightly as they weep. They know that this is not a just whimsical piece of

public art in the shadow of Hungary's Parliament, near the dozens of tour boats that ply the river between Buda and Pest. Three plaques—in Hungarian, English, and Hebrew—explaining

what the shoes represent are embedded in the walkway well behind the shoes, so it is easily possible for passersby not to realize what they symbolize. The inscriptions on the plaques read: "To the memory of the victims shot into the Danube by Arrow Cross militiamen in 1944-45. Erected 16 April 2005."

This is, in fact, a Holocaust memorial entitled *Shoes along the Danube Promenade*, in memory of 20,000 people—mostly Jews—who were rounded up in 1944–5, marched to the banks of the Danube, and stripped of their clothes, including their shoes. Then they were shot by the Arrow Cross, the Hungarian equivalent of the Nazis, and their bodies fell or were thrown into the river. The

memorial, designed by film director Can Togay and created by sculptor Gyula Pauer, consists of sixty pairs of period-appropriate shoes made out of iron, attached to the stone embankment. The sculptor chose iron because it has little value and would not be of interest to thieves, but vandals have pried some of the shoes loose and—in a macabre echo of history—thrown them into the river.

The simplicity of the memorial and the beauty of its location make it all the more moving and powerful.

When I saw the little children's shoes on the banks of the Danube, I was devastated. I immediately thought of my nieces, Sarah's children. When I saw the high-buckled shoes, I thought of my mom. It took me back to 1927, when I was around three years of age, and my mom was sitting on the bed buckling up her shoes, getting ready to go to the hospital. She was very sick after my youngest sister Fradel was born, and she had to have a hysterectomy. When she got off the bed and put on her brown coat with the yellow lining in it, I stood against the door so she couldn't go out. Remembering that broke me up while I looked at the shoes.

I thought about how there could be human beings who can hate to that degree. When my granddaughter Alexandra was eight, she asked me if I had any sisters or brothers. I said yes. "Did they die in the war?" I said yes, except for my sister Sarah. "Did she have any children?" Yes. "Did they die in the war?" Yes. Then she said, "What kind of people can hurt children?" The only answer I could think of was, "People who hate."

3

SATU MARE

When we come back to a place, we want to come back to what it was, not what it is now. I wanted to find some trace of my family, the places we lived in, the stores we shopped in. That's what I saw in the back of my mind, but when I went there, I didn't find it. It was as if we had never been there.

Eva Olsson

Satu Mare is a city of 160,421, situated on the Szamos River in northwest Romania, 13 kilometres from the border with Hungary and 27 kilometres from the border with the Ukraine. The population is 58% Romanian and 35% Hungarian, reflecting the fact that at one time it was part of Hungary, and was called Szatmar.

The Jews of Hungary, especially those in the northwest, didn't feel too threatened by the war that had started in Europe in 1939, as they thought it would end soon. They were hearing stories of terrible things happening to Jews in Poland and Czechoslovakia, but had no way of knowing if they were true.

On June 27th, 1941, after Germany had invaded the Soviet Union, Hungary formally declared war against the Soviet Union and became a full Axis partner to Germany and Italy. In 1944, when Russian troops were approaching Hungary, Germany was worried that Hungary might change sides, so they invaded it on March 19, 1944. Adolph Eichmann was put in charge of deporting and eliminating the Hungarian Jews as quickly as possible. The deportations from Satu Mare began on May 15, 1944.

According to reports kept by the Germans, the number of Jews deported from Hungary within two days of the start of the operation on May 15 was 23,363. By May 18, it reached about 51,000. By June 7, within twenty-four days of starting, they had deported 289,357 Jews in ninety-two trains—a daily average of 12,056 people deported and an average of 3,145 per train.

The non-stop train trip from Budapest to Satu Mare took seven hours, through pleasant, mostly rural, countryside. We arrived in the dark around eight in the evening to find the station almost deserted. It took us a while to find a taxi large to take us and our luggage to our hotel, a task made more difficult by the fact that all the Romanian banks were closed and we only had Hungarian money. Although both Hungary and Romania are part of the European Union (EU), neither has yet adopted the euro as its currency. However, we found a man who agreed to accept 1,000 Hungarian forints (about $6) and had a large vehicle, so we made it to the hotel.

We spent the next day, Sunday, walking around the area Eva had known as a child, trying to find streets she had walked then. It didn't help that the street signs were now in Romanian, not Hungarian. We also found that many of the streets no longer existed, and most of the buildings Eva would have know had been torn down and replaced.

We found the registry office where Eva hoped to find records of birthdates and birthplaces of the members of her family, as well as her sister Sarah's married name. The people there were really helpful, scurrying back and forth between offices with files. In the end, Eva got the information she wanted.

The reason I never wanted to go back to Satu Mare was fear. I was afraid that nothing from my birthplace and childhood would be there. I was afraid I wouldn't find anything—and I didn't. My fears had been valid. I was more devastated than you will ever know.

My family was living in one room when I was born and stayed there until I was twenty months of age. Then we moved to 36 Petofi Street, to a place with two rooms, a veranda, and a small garden. Three other families shared a courtyard with us—the Jonas family, Mindy and her daughter Rosa, and the Hermann couple. Going back to that neighbourhood, I hoped the gate might still be there and we could have gone inside the courtyard. It would have been a connection with my past. But there was nothing left of any of the houses I had lived in! Nothing! A new post office is being built where our house used to be.

When I was 14, we rented a bungalow a block away from our two-room apartment. This place was on Halas Ferency Street, at the corner of Bathory Boulevard, across from the grocery store. Although it was quite small, it had two rooms and a kitchen. Our landlord, Mr Lefcovich, lived in a new bungalow beside us. When I was in Sweden after the war, I found out from someone that he had survived. The school around the corner is still there, but the other buildings had all been replaced.

Except for the park and the school, there wasn't one place where I could say, "Yes, I recognize this, I recognize that, that's where I played." All the synagogues my family used to go to are gone. The one my mother used to attend was torn down a month before we arrived. I spoke to a man in the street who turned out to be Jewish and was on his way to celebrate the 200th anniversary of a synagogue, so there's at least one left in the city. Out of 13,000 Jewish inhabitants, only 20 elderly Jewish families live in Satu Mare now. There was very little evidence that such a large Jewish population had ever even been there, or what had happened to them. After the way they were treated by Romanians during the deportations, it's not surprising that very few Jews went back to Romania after the war. In fact, it wasn't that long ago that the Romanian government was denying that the Holocaust had even happened there.

All I am left with are my memories of the way it used to be.

I talked with three Roma (Gypsy) men on the street, asking them what had happened to Petofi Street and Bathory Boulevard. We talked about Auschwitz-Birkenau and how

many Gypsies died there too. None of these men were alive at that time, but they said they knew that the Nazis had considered Gypsies to be inferior too and had exterminated over 500,000 of them in concentration camps. When I was young, my Uncle Wolf, my mother's brother, used to call me *Cigainer*, (Gypsy in Hungarian), probably because of my curly dark hair and eyes. And maybe because of my free spirit too.

When I was young and used to walk along the Szamos River near our home, there were lovely cafes and restaurants there. I used to walk there and listen to the music that was playing, something we never had at home. That's how I learned some of the songs the musicians played at the restaurant in Budapest. The road along the river was still there, but it has been built up now to stop flooding and is very scruffy, not beautiful the way it used to be. There are no longer any cafes or restaurants along that part of the river. The last time I had been there was when we were taken away by the Nazis.

On May 15, 1944, a man came, stood in the square, banged on a drum, and read from a piece of paper, "You've got two hours to pack your bags with enough clothing for two weeks. No food. Leave your money, jewelry, and valuables in the house. You're going to a work camp, a brick factory in Germany." We wanted to take things with us that were special to us, that meant something to us. Sarah's wedding ring and my mom's were thrown up on the roof, into the eavestrough, so they could find them when they came back. I guess it didn't occur to them that when it rained the rings might be washed down the drainpipes.

They also dug up a place under the floorboards and buried things there that Regina's husband, Sandelman, had got from his parents. At that time, Regina was in the hospital, which was in a house across from 36 Petofi Street. Fradel told me when I met her in Boston in 1982 that Sandelman survived, got remarried, and lives in New York. I don't know if he ever went back to Satu Mare and looked for these things, or if they were discovered before the war was over.

We packed our bags and lined up with our families, five people to a row. Included in our family group were Sarah's three children and my brother Martin, his wife, and their little baby. My sister Regina had to stay behind in the ghetto hospital because her six-month-old baby girl had the measles. We learned later that the patients from this hospital were evacuated and taken directly to the gas chamber.

We were marched to the train station where my brother Lazar and I had tried to help the people on the freight trains. In late February 1944, we heard that freight trains containing thousands of Jews were passing through our town, so Lazar and I started going to people's homes late at night and collecting food. We took the food by horse and buggy to the station, hoping that the people who owned the hotel beside the railway station could get the food to the people on the trains. It did not occur to us that later that year we would be marched to the station and jammed into boxcars ourselves.

It took us a long time to get there because they made us walk—
the final walk—seven kilometres along the road by the river to
be transported to Auschwitz-Birkenau. They probably took us
along the backroads rather than through the city because they
didn't want the people to see what was going on. But many
Hungarians were lined up along the road as we marched the
seven kilometers to the train station, and the Hungarian police
and military both co-operated with the Germans. I couldn't
understand why Hungarians were not only allowing the
Germans to do this to us but were also assisting them. I still
remember seeing our dentist, standing by the bridge, watching
us go by. I often wonder what he was thinking.

The park opposite the Dacia Hotel was also diminished from the time I lived there; the rose arbour where lovers used to sit was gone, although there were still roses there. I spoke to two older women who were sitting in the park, and they told me that life in Romania is hard. Their pensions are very small, and unemployment is high. I used to love sneaking into the opera house and being mesmerized by the beautiful drapes, and the red and gold chairs. But the elegance and beauty of the opera house was all gone too—no velvet drapes or murals—probably destroyed by one government or another. Satu Mare was like a café where the food was good, but had no flavour for me. The Jewish spirit of the city was missing; the merchants that used to be there were gone—the jeweller, textile merchants, bank, delicatessen, the shoe store by the Dacia Hotel.

The Dacia Hotel is still there, opposite the park. It looked good, but the lobby wasn't as impressive as I remembered. When I was a teenager, I had my picture taken at a photographer's shop in a lane near the hotel, wearing a turtleneck sweater, with my hair curled like Shirley Temple's. I hid the picture because my parents' religious beliefs forbid such things; I wanted it just for me. We were poor, but I got the money to pay the photographer by helping a family who owned a dry goods store that sold ties, shirts, socks, winter long johns, that type of thing. They were a nice couple, orthodox, but not Hasidic like us. They used to give me a little money for helping sort things and put them on the shelf.

I also used to help Mrs. Weiss, the baker's wife. When they made cakes for weddings, I would stir the eggs and the sugar until it was yellow and thick. Her mother and my mother grew up in the same courtyard, so there was a connection between our families. The baker was a nice Jewish Orthodox man. She was a big woman and he was a short man. She told the people who owned the grocery store that I was an unpolished diamond. My mother wondered why they liked me better than Regina. At that point I realized I was different from my sisters Regina and Sarah, and my brother Martin. I was definitely different than Fradel. It made me happy to know that people liked me, and I was always eager to do things for them, like running errands. Because of their religion, my parents couldn't see the positive qualities that others saw in me or Lazar.

When I turned ten, Rosa, a modern Jewish woman who lived next door, bought me white chrysanthemums. My mother wondered why she would do that, as Hasidic people don't celebrate birthdays. I was very surprised but pleased to receive such a gift on my birthday, and chrysanthemums are still my favourite flowers. The Jonas family next door had three sons that were adults and one daughter, Fagi. She showed me how to give myself a manicure to make my nails look nice. Behind the hotel was a place where you could go and buy ice cream and sweets. When my Uncle Wolf visited, he'd give me some change and I would run and buy either an ice cream or a slice of Dobos torte and eat it up before I got home. Those were happy times, good memories.

As I got older, my parents began to suspect that I was not going to follow their religious ways. My youngest sister constantly squealed on me; she was what we call a bully today. If I fixed my hair on the Sabbath, or looked out the window, she'd tell my parents and I'd get spanked the next day. Fradel was a bully then, and she still is today, trying to control my life.

I wanted to find the Jewish cemetery where my maternal grandfather, whom I never knew, and my grandmother, whom I did know, were buried, so I could visit their graves. I knew it was near the railway station because I had gone there with my mother and placed stones on their graves. We found a couple of cemeteries, but neither was the right one. A woman offered to walk us to the right place. Like most other Jewish

sites, the gate was locked, so she went to a house across the street to get the man who had the key to the gate. He wasn't home, so we all we could do was look over the fence and take some pictures. Even though I couldn't place a stone, I'm sure they will know I was there and that they are not forgotten.

In Satu Mare we did find some compassionate people who helped us, people like Johanna Riedl Kovacs at the city archives and Dr. Cucuiet Lucian, the Director of National Archives. Johanna and her staff managed to find the birthdates of all my siblings, information I had not had before then. She had tears in her eyes as she hugged me and said goodbye. Dr. Lucian kissed my hand when he met me, and he helped fill out a form requesting information about my mother's birthplace. I received this information in the mail a few months later.

The night after I had walked along the river road, I woke up and cried a flood. Not finding any of the homes where we had lived, or my grandmother's place or Sarah's house was devastating for me. My worst fears had come true: There was no trace that my family had ever been there. As beautiful as Satu Mare might be to others, it wasn't beautiful to me anymore.

When I got on the train to leave Satu Mare, only part of me was on that train; another part of me was in the boxcar, 63 years ago. I saw my father and my two brothers standing there. I saw my mom sitting in a corner, hugging her three grandchildren, Sarah's children. Sixty-three years later, as we headed for Poland, I was still seeing my family taking their final journey on those same tracks.

Satu Mare

4

SIGHET

I know now that I have walked the streets where my father and grandfather walked.

Eva Olsson

Located in Maramures County, in northern Transylvania, on the border with the Ukraine, Sighet (Sighetu Marmatiei) is a city of 44,000 surrounded by small villages. This relatively isolated area has one of the most intact peasant cultures of Europe, with rich ethnographic and folklore elements. The men are skillful wood carvers, as can be seen in the carved wooden gates at each home, and a man's prestige in the village is determined by the size and elaborateness of his carved front gate. All the old houses and churches are entirely

made of wood. The women sit by the gates of their houses spinning wool with which they weave clothes and blankets.

Being there is like stepping back a hundred years, with people scything the hay and gathering it with homemade wooden rakes.

Going to Sighet was important to Eva because she had never been to the place where her favourite grandfather lived. A planned trip there when she was eleven had been aborted by her father, and Eva was determined not to miss seeing it this time.

Making travel arrangements to get from Satu Mare to Sighet and back was one of the most difficult parts of the trip-planning process. Although they are just over two hours apart by car, it was hard to get accurate information as to the best way to make the trip. One Romanian travel agency I contacted sent me the timetable for an eight-hour trip on three different trains. Rob Larcombe, whom I contacted on ThornTree on the Internet, told me about a van that ran between the two towns once a day, but when we tried to make reservations, we were told it was first come, first served. Information about the van and its schedule was very sketchy, even when we were in Satu Mare, and that was making me nervous. As we had reserved seats on four different trains for the 21-hour journey to Krakow, Poland, and hotel reservations once we got there, we had to be sure we could not only get to Sighet, but also get back to Satu Mare in three days to catch the first train. Rob told me that he could probably line up a ride back, so first we had to get to Sighet.

We were having lunch in an outdoor café the second day after we had arrived in Satu Mare, and Eva struck up a conversation in Hungarian with our waitress. When Eva mentioned the difficulty we were having getting to Sighet, the waitress said she had a friend—Carman, a waiter at the same café —who might be willing to drive us. She phoned him and he agreed to take us the next day for 50 euros, in a taxi he would borrow from a friend.

The next day we left our large luggage at the hotel and packed smaller bags with what we'd need for the three days we'd be in Sighet. We met Carman at the café around noon, loaded up the cab, and set off. It was a bright, sunny day, and the drive was thoroughly enjoyable. After going through a few small towns, we began the climb up to the pass over the mountain that separates the two valleys. The road switchbacked many times, providing us with wonderful views as we twisted and turned. At one point we stopped to photograph a couple who were scything their hayfield. They gladly posed for Don and me, and the woman scribbled her name and address on a piece

of paper so I could send her a copy of the picture. Unfortunately, I can't read what she wrote.

Before we reached Sighet, Carman took a short detour to show us what the guidebooks call the "Merry Cemetery" in the village of Sapanta. The name reflects both the colourful grave markers and the fact that the villagers view death not as a tragedy, but as a passage to a better place. The tombstones marking the graves are made of carved oak and consist of a verse written as if it was spoken by the deceased, along with a brightly painted picture of the person in daily life or at the moment of death. The tradition of carving wooden grave markers and

writing a short verse was started in1935 by Stan Ioan Patras, a local carver. He got the inspiration for his short verses by eavesdropping on gossip and listening to stories at the wake, where the relatives of the dead person do not mourn, but drink and make merry. There are few secrets in such a small town.

One grave marker shows a three-year-old girl being hit by a car. The verse reads:

Burn in Hell you
damned Taxi

That came from Sibiu.

As large as Romania is

You couldn't find any
other place to stop

Only in front of
my house

To kill me?

When Patras died in 1977, Dumitru Pop, his apprentice, took over and continues in this role today. The cemetery paints a picture of life in the village throughout its history, often revealing the peoples' flaws as well as their strengths.

The picture on another marker shows a man who loved his horses, but the verse includes a telling detail:

One more thing I loved very much,

To sit at a table in a bar

Next to someone else's wife.

Another man's verse reads:

Underneath this heavy cross

Lies my mother-in-law poor.

Had she lived three days more

I would be here and she would read.

You that are passing by

Try not to wake her up,

For if she comes back home

She'll bite my head off.

But I will act in the way

That she will not return.

Stay here my dear

Mother-in-law.

The pictures are simple—the housewife, the carpenter, the woodcutter, and the spinner are depicted alongside the drunk, the lecherous man, and the man who loved the Communist Party most of all.

The cemetery has become a major tourist attraction in the area, charging admission and selling a guide to the tombstones. It is well named, for we found ourselves smiling and chuckling as we walked around. Not a bad way to be remembered.

We met Rob Larcombe in Sighet, across the road from Cobwobs, the hostel he and Lia run. It got its name from the fact that Lia, a Romanian, couldn't pronounce the word "cobwebs"; it always came out "cobwobs." The chalet-style hostel is set back from the road behind a flourishing garden that's tended by Lia's mother, Maria, who lives with her husband on the ground floor of the hostel. Rob got us settled in our rooms, and then took us for a drive around Sighet.

The first stop was the railway station, which sits about 500 metres from the Ukrainian border. One unnerving detail was the winged symbol at the front of the station that looked very

much like the German eagle. Apparently the station was relatively unchanged from the days when thousands of Jews—including Eva's favourite grandfather Jankev, and Nobel Peace Prize winner Elie Wiesel and his family—were shipped to Auschwitz-Birkenau. The station was very quiet, except for three or four people sitting on a bench alongside the tracks. Rob told us not to pay too much attention to them or photograph them, as they were probably smugglers, bringing goods in from the Ukraine, where everything—especially cigarettes—was much cheaper. We pointedly ignored them.

Then we went to the Holocaust memorial by the Jewish graveyard. It is a large black marble structure with Romanian and Hebrew writing on it, commemorating the thousands of Jews who were shipped to concentration camps. It sits beside a large weeping willow tree, reminiscent of the sculpture behind

the synagogue in Budapest. The memorial sits amidst uncut grass, behind a locked gate and wrought-iron fence, so we couldn't get near to it.

Rob introduced us to Ioan (Johnny) Popescu, a local journalist who has written a history of the Jews of Sighet. Although he's not Jewish, Johnny said he worked on this project "because it needed to be done." He joined us for dinner the night we arrived, and spent the next day walking us around Sighet, giving Eva a tour of the place her grandfather would have known. His help was invaluable, and made the visit to Sighet one of the highlights of our trip.

My Grandfather Jankev (my father's father), whom I loved dearly, lived in the city of Sighet, in an area formerly known as Northern Transylvania. He made his living sewing the leather tops of custom-made shoes, and his family worked a small farm. My Grandmother Rifka died at an early age, when my father was about twenty-two, and is buried in the Jewish cemetery in Sighet. My grandfather remarried, to a widow with two adult children who were so modern they didn't speak a word of Yiddish. My father's stepbrother looked like a man who just walked out of Vogue magazine. When he came to visit us in Satu Mare, he stayed at the Dacia Hotel. His sister was beautiful, like a madonna from Spain.

I always loved my Grandfather Jankev more than my father and my memories of him are all positive. He was generous, caring, lovable, and wise—the opposite of my father. He was Orthodox, but not Hasidic like my father. He wore a different hat than my father did. He wore a grey suit, not the long black coats Hasidic men like my father wore. He was a very gentle man, short, with a long beard that had some auburn in it, and he wore glasses. He was very quiet, a pleasant, jolly man, always playing around with the kids, a good male influence for me. It was a joy to have him visit because he'd play old Yiddish melodies on his violin. He also brought us goodies: walnuts, hazelnuts, and a huge honey cake my step-grandmother would make, as well as a big chunk of homemade butter his wife had made.

The happiest time of my life was when my grandfather came to visit. My father behaved differently when my grandfather was there. He was on his best behaviour. Remembering those times brings me both sadness and joy.

When I was about eleven and a half, my mother decided to send me to my Sighet for a little holiday. It was a chance for me to visit my grandfather, my step-grandmother, and my father's stepsister, Ester, without the company of any other siblings. At the time, my father was out of town, travelling to different Jewish communities and synagogues promoting his books. Since I had never been to my favourite grandfather's home, I eagerly packed my suitcase for the six-hour trip to Sighet. My grandparents were going to pick me up at the train station.

However, my father came home before Mama was expecting him and said I could not go. He said he was worried that I might fall into the fast-moving river near my grandfather's house. I was so upset I cried all night. We didn't have a telephone, so we couldn't let my grandparents know I wasn't coming, and they waited at the train station for a long time. My father sent them a letter saying that I wasn't going to go there for that summer holiday.

As it turned out this would have been my only chance to see where my grandparents lived. I never saw Grandfather Jankev again after I turned 18, because the Jews of Sighet were taken to Auschwitz-Birkenau in the spring of 1944. At that time he would have been around 70 years old, so he and his wife

54

would have been taken directly to the gas chambers. I don't know what happened to his stepson and stepdaughter.

Seventy-three years later, I had the opportunity to go and see where my grandfather lived. But he wasn't there this time… nobody from my family was there. Johnny spent the whole day with us, sharing his knowledge of the history of the Jewish community in Sighet. As we were walking around, Johnny pointed out buildings where the Jewish merchants used to live, and talked about how they struggled to survive. Most of them were poor people. Johnny said that we were walking on streets that my grandfather and father would have walked on many times. I felt that their spirit was there, and I hope my grandfather knew I was there.

When we went to the synagogue, Hari Markus, the head of the Jewish community in Sighet, gave us a brief history of what had happened there. We looked at old record books to see if there were any Maleks there, relatives on my father's side of the family. We did find a Henrick Malek listed, but when we checked his stone in the graveyard, it wasn't possible to tell if there was any connection with our family.

We met some very caring people there too. We stayed at Cobwobs, Lia and Rob's hostel, and they made our stay there very enjoyable. Rob drove us to several villages outside Sighet to see the wooden churches and gates, and we stopped at a monastery as well. It was nice to see the mountains I used to hear my parents talk about.

Rob ended up driving us back to Satu Mare at the end of our visit, solving that problem for us as well. Lia's mother, Maria, wanted to provide us with supper one night, and we feasted on cabbage rolls she made. They helped make our visit to Sighet very warm and friendly.

When we went to the Jewish Cemetery, I was hoping to find the grave of Rifka Malek, my father's mother, who died at a young age, before any of her grandchildren were born. The gate to the Jewish cemetery was locked, but we could see workers cutting the grass inside. Rob went across the street and summoned a woman who had the key. I knew approximately when my grandmother had died, so a young man who was working there got some photocopied sheets and we began to look for my grandmother's name. Then he led us to a back corner of the cemetery, where he pointed to two crumbling gravestones and said they might be the right ones, although the writing on them could not be read.

When I was a little girl in Satu Mare I went with my mom to the Jewish cemetery on the other side of the railway station. She picked up two little stones and put one on my grandmother's grave and one on my grandfather's. At the time I didn't think about why she did that. Years later, I asked a friend and she didn't know either. So I put stones on the two old gravestones the young man thought might be my grandmother's. I figured that if my grandmother lies there, she'll know that I had remembered her. I had never known her, yet it was very emotional for me to be there. I noticed that many of the other tombstones had the weeping willow symbol on them. Not surprisingly, many tombstones commemorated people who perished in Auschwitz-Birkenau.

At one point Johnny stopped in front of an apartment building to show us a gravesite. To get into the yard of the building, he buzzed for a lady to come down and let us in. The grave belongs to a famous rabbi from the 17th century, and has an interesting story connected to it. Years ago, when they were moving the cemetery in order to build the apartment building, lightning struck as they were trying to move this last grave, so they left it alone. The myth grew that the grave couldn't ever be moved. Now it sits beside the building, tended by Olimpia and Georghe Iancu, who live in the building.

When we were standing by the grave, Johnny said to me, "It's a miracle that you're here." When we parted at the end of the day, I said to him, "Keep up the good work," and he said, "This isn't work. Somebody has to do it." It's not that often that you come across someone who is so dedicated to a cause, to keeping the history of the Jewish people in Maramures alive. I'm grateful to him and I'll always remember him. Should my journey take me back there again, I hope we'll connect again.

After we visited the gravesite, the Iancus invited us into their apartment. She didn't speak Hungarian, but her husband did. Their apartment was typical of an eastern European home. As soon as we were settled, out came the goodies—coffee, cakes, and a plum brandy that was very strong. Gheorghe had been the director of a factory that made fancy furniture, and he gave me a book showing all the chairs they made. We talked about what life was like in Romania now. I will always remember his face as we were leaving. His face was red and his eyes were wet. He was very emotional. This was good to see, because in spite of the fact that a lot of atrocities had happened in that area, there were good people there who were very kind. Perhaps that's why I'm drawn to go back there. I was sad that I didn't find that in my hometown, Satu Mare.

I was very happy with our visit to Sighet. It's a beautiful area, and something is drawing me back. I feel there might be more for me to discover there, moreso than in my birthplace. I know there's no one from our family left in Satu Mare. Maybe I hope I'll find a piece of the puzzle—some link to relatives who survived the Holocaust—in Sighet, or nearby Baia Mare (Nagybánya in Hungarian), where my grandfather once lived and where my father was born. I don't even know how many relatives I had there, but perhaps I could find records that might tell me that. Prior to the war there were about 15,000 Jews in and around the city. Now there are only about 100 Jews living there. That's better than Satu Mare, which only has 20 Jewish families left.

5

AUSCHWITZ-BIRKENAU

Forever let this place be a cry of despair
and a warning to humanity.

Plaque on memorial at Auschwitz-Birkenau

The truth is that in this place, we have all the
reason in the world to give up on humanity,
but we will not give up on humanity. We have
all the reason in the world to choose anger, and
we shall not yield to anger. Hope is all we
have, and hope is all we can give one another.

Elie Wiesel

Auschwitz-Birkenau is not just any place.

It has become a symbol of terror, genocide, and the Holocaust—the "Final Solution of the Jewish Question"—the Nazi plan to exterminate every one of the 11 million Jews of Europe. According to train records, 1.3 million Jews were brought to Auschwitz-Birkenau, in German-occupied Poland, and 200,000 were transferred to other camps. Based on these figures, at least 1.1 million Jews were murdered there, along with 75,000 Poles, and some 19,000 Roma (Gypsies), making Auschwitz-Birkenau the site of the greatest mass murder in history, as well as the world's largest Jewish graveyard, with the ashes of over a million victims scattered there.

When the Soviet Army liberated Auschwitz-Birkenau on January 27, 1945, they found 7,600 survivors. In the preceding weeks, the Nazis had evacuated more than 58,000 prisoners and sent them on final death marches to Germany.

The town of Auschwitz, 38 miles from Krakow, was founded by Germans in 1270, but in 1457 it became part of the Kingdom of Poland and was known by its Polish name, Oswiecim. The Germans invaded Poland on September 1, 1939 and captured Oswiecim on September 6. They renamed the town Auschwitz and proceeded to establish three separate prison camps just outside the town:

Auschwitz I, established in April 1940, was primarily a transit camp and administrative center, although over 70,000 people died there;

Auschwitz II (Birkenau) built in 1941–1942, was an extermination camp;

Auschwitz III (Monowitz) was a labour camp, one of 40 established in that area and known collectively as Auschwitz III.

In June 2007, the World Heritage Committee approved Poland's request to change the name of Auschwitz on UNESCO's World Heritage List from "Auschwitz Concentration Camp" to "Auschwitz-Birkenau," with the subtitle "German Nazi Concentration and Extermination Camp (1940-1945)." The Polish people resent Auschwitz-Birkenau being described as a concentration camp in Poland. They want people to remember that during the time that Auschwitz-Birkenau was a killing center, it was part of the Greater German Reich, not Poland.

The world first learned that the Jews were being gassed when resistance fighters in the Polish Underground passed this information on to the Polish government-in-exile in Great Britain. On June 25, 1942, The Telegraph, *a British newspaper, ran a story about the mass murder of Jews in gas chambers at Auschwitz-Birkenau. The headline read "Germans murder 700,000 Jews in Poland." This story was also broadcast over the BBC. The killings continued for the next two years and seven months.*

The train trip from Satu Mare to Krakow was the most demanding one of the journey, as it consisted of taking four trains over a 21-hour period. We left Satu Mare at 8:15 AM on September 27, arrived in Valea lui Mihai at 9:40; left there at 11:15 and arrived in Debrecen at noon; left there at 1 and arrived in Miskolc at 2:30. We had a six-hour stopover there and took an overnight train to Krakow, arriving there at 5:15 AM.

Our tickets on this last nine-hour part of the trip turned out to be second class, and the compartment, which had exactly six non-reclining seats in it, already had a young couple sitting there. As soon as we had stashed our luggage in the upper racks, I went looking for the first-class section, located several empty compartments, flagged down the conductor (who spoke no English), dragged him back to speak Hungarian with Eva, paid him 10 euros, and moved us to first class, where each of us tried to get as comfortable as possible for the long journey. I'm told that some of us were more successful at this than others.

To add to the fun, we passed through several borders—Hungary, Slovak Republic, Poland—and were awakened by gun-toting customs officers who asked to see our passports. Well, that's what we assumed they were shouting, in various languages, none of them English. At one point after a customs agent had left with our passports, I decided to step out of the compartment into the corridor for a stretch. When I did so, a soldier at the end of the car waved me back—with his machine gun—into the compartment. He didn't need to ask me twice.

We arrived in a damp, foggy Krakow around 5:30 a.m. and checked into the Chopin Hotel—after a long detour on foot, dragging our wheeled luggage, around a major road construction project. After a few hours sleep, a shower, and some breakfast, we set off in a tour bus for the concentration camp.

We decided to take a commercial tour to visit Auschwitz-Birkenau, and that proved to be a very wise decision, as it allowed Eva to revisit the camps without feeling she had to act as our guide. The 50-kilometre bus trip from Krakow to Auschwitz takes about two hours, through lush, green countryside, dotted with prosperous-looking, well-maintained houses. It might have been a pleasant journey under different circumstances, but our destination was uppermost in our minds and that precluded enjoying the scenery.

As we were driving along, a film was playing on the small screen at the front of the bus, and everyone on the bus was watching silently, with solemn faces. The film was a documentary about the concentration camps at our destination—Auschwitz-Birkenau—and it provided a jarring contrast to the pastoral countryside we were travelling through. When the graphic images on the screen got to be too much to look at, all we had to do was turn our heads and look out the windows at a very different Poland than the one on the screen.

Three thousand people a day visit Auschwitz-Birkenau, so arrival there is a somewhat hectic scene, not quite as solemn and sober as one might want or expect. Most people come on tour buses, as we did, so Kate, our young Polish tour guide, gave us last-minute instructions as to what time we would be heading back to Krakow and how to figure out which bus was ours. When she was handing out the stickers that would identify the members of her tour group, I told her that Eva was a survivor of the camps. She glanced over at Eva and then back to me, her face registering the fact that this would not be just a routine tour of hell for her. She handed one sticker to me; Eva would not need one.

Don and I needed special permission to be able to film inside buildings at the camp, so Kate got on her cell phone and made the necessary arrangements. We were given special stickers to wear, but even with those, we were very careful not to intrude on other peoples' experience as they toured the camp.

We would wait until people had moved on before taking any pictures. The only place where absolutely no photography was allowed—understandably—was in the gas chamber.

All the tours start at Auschwitz I, where about 28 of the original two-storey brick buildings still stand and have been converted to accommodate displays relating to different aspects of what happened to prisoners after they arrived there. Signs above the entrances to these buildings gave us a stark indication of what we were going to find inside: Extermination ... Material Proofs of Crimes ... Prisoners' Life. Other buildings weren't open to the public, but signs posted by the doors indicated what had happened in them: sterilization experiments on women, medical experiments on children, torture and killing of political prisoners and resistance fighters—a grim litany of horror that seemed endless.

Rudolf Hoess had the "*Arbeit Macht Frei*" sign installed over the entrance into Auschwitz I. In English, the words mean "Work will set you free." In his autobiography, Hoess explained that this expression means that work liberates one in the spiritual sense, not that the prisoners literally had a chance of being released if they worked hard—a distinction that was probably lost on the prisoners entering through that gate.

Many other group tours were being conducted simultaneously with ours, so there were often line-ups at the entrances to buildings, on staircases, and in display rooms. But this was all conducted in hushed voices, with people shuffling sombrely from place to place, trying to stay in touch with their tour groups without pushing or bumping into other people. At times it was a very claustrophobic experience. After a while a kind of numbness set in, as if the brain could not process one more detail of the depravity that had happened there.

And then there would be something that would cause a viewer to gasp or stop dead or clutch a friend's arm for support. One of those moments was the pile of suitcases—thousands of them—with names and hometowns written on them. People had been told to do this so they'd be able to find their own suitcases after they'd been through the "showers." They encouraged people to go quickly to

the showers: "Raus! Raus! Hurry up. Get in there. When you come out you will have coffee." These are not just anonymous artifacts of history. There are people's names on them. People had packed these suitcases in their homes, after carefully deciding what were the most important possessions they had. They had been told they were being relocated and should leave all their money and jewelry behind. It was heartbreaking to read the names so carefully printed on each suitcase by owners who had no idea what was about to happen to them.

After we finished the tour of Auschwitz I, we boarded our bus for the three-kilometre trip to Auschwitz II, commonly referred to as Birkenau. The Birkenau camp is huge: 425 acres, with boundaries stretching a mile in one direction and a mile and a half in the other. At its peak size, there were over 300 buildings there, able to accommodate 200,000 prisoners, making it the largest concentration camp in the entire Nazi system. It had been designed and built as an extermination camp, a death factory for gassing Jews, with two very large underground gas chambers, two smaller gas chambers, plus two old farmhouses that were used for gassing as well.

The guided tour of Birkenau consisted mainly of viewing a typical barrack that had housed prisoners, and a latrine building. After that we were free to walk about on our own and encouraged to walk along the train tracks from the main gate to the memorial where the tracks stopped. On either side of the tracks at this point are the remains of the gas chambers and crematoria. Eva wanted  to spend more time at Birkenau, so we told Kate that we wouldn't be taking the tour bus back to Krakow, but would be using the local bus service.

The Auschwitz-Birkenau memorial, entitled the "International Monument to the Victims of Fascism," was dedicated in 1967, after hundreds of other designs had been considered and rejected over the preceding decade. The memorial is an abstract stone construction surrounded by steps and plaques in many languages, with the inscription:

> Forever let this place be a cry of despair
>
> and a warning to humanity,
>
> where the Nazis murdered
>
> about one and a half million men,
>
> women and children,
>
> mainly Jews,
>
> from various countries of Europe.

Although the memorial is the central focus at the end of the tracks, it doesn't register with visitors as much as the designers probably intended. However, it is hard to imagine that any memorial could make a statement stronger than that made by the twisted concrete and girder ruins of Krema II and Krema III, the two largest crematoria, which lie on either side of it behind barbed wire.

I'm glad I came back to Auschwitz-Birkenau, but it was devastating. I felt like someone had taken the air out of me … like a burst balloon … hollow, empty. The whole thing was overpowering … the fact that I was there. The video they showed on the bus brought it all back.

In spite of all the people around you, you are still alone. I was determined to stay in control that day. I welcomed the rain that was falling when we were at the camp—the tears of those who can't cry anymore.

Kate, our Polish tour guide at Auschwitz-Birkenau, was such a beautiful soul, a very caring human being. You could tell she was touched. Several times on the tour she spoke to me and said, "If you need to leave the tour I will understand." She told me that she found it very depressing, very difficult to do this work. She didn't know how much longer she could conduct the tours. Maybe two more years, but no longer than that. She also told me that sometimes Nazis come on her tours and shout, "This is a lie. It never happened."

As she was giving us details about the camp, I was thinking about when I was there, what it was like. And I was thinking about how there is so much information out there that most people will never hear or see.

Kate really knew what she was doing; she was very good at it. It touched me that she hugged me at the end of the tour, turned away, then came back and hugged me again, and she was crying. I took her hand and thanked her for doing such a good job, and she got very emotional and turned away.

When we arrived in Auschwitz-Birkenau on May 19, 1944, we got out and stood beside the train tracks—a mass of luggage, prisoners, guard dogs, barbed wire, electric fences, and high towers with machine guns and SS troops on them. Some prisoners in striped suits tried to help us, saying, "Raus, Raus"

("Get out quickly, get out"). People were relieved to be getting out of the boxcars, expecting to get food and water and breathe fresh air. There was no food and water for us. My brain was numb with fear ... horrendous fear and shock. *What's going on here? Why are we here? There's no brick factory here.* It was beyond description.

The air was filled with an awful stench, a horrible smell that reminded me of when we burned the last feathers off of chickens after we had plucked them. The sky was black from the smoke coming out of the five tall chimneys. In Satu Mare they had told us they were taking us to a brick factory, but they took us to a killing factory. We had no idea what was going on or that this was part of something as enormous as the Holocaust. I realized later how little I knew when I was there. There was no "outside" anymore. There was only survival—*How can I make it to the next day?*

Seeing pictures of individual prisoners and the piles of toothbrushes, shoes, hair, and suitcases brings the horror down to a more personal level. It's no longer about numbers in the millions; it's about people we can identify with. The memorial plaques on the wall also helped make the deaths more personal.

Three things really hit me when I visited Auschwitz-Birkenau this time. First was the train tracks leading into Birkenau. For 75 percent of those who arrived on these tracks, there was no return. The main gate at Birkenau took me right back to that time. I saw a boxcar … my father and brother standing … my mother squatting.

The walk along the track to the memorial was important to me because that's how the victims arrived. After July 8, 1944 there was no more selection; everyone went straight to the gas chambers. The tracks were extended so they were closer to the crematorium.

Second were the piles of shoes. Tens of thousands of shoes.

There had been people who walked in those shoes— children, old people, mothers and fathers. Somehow seeing the piles of shoes makes you realize that these people had lives, histories, dreams that were taken from them. The children had not even had time to develop their personalities. They were robbed. And the thought crosses my mind: Did any of those shoes belong to my family?

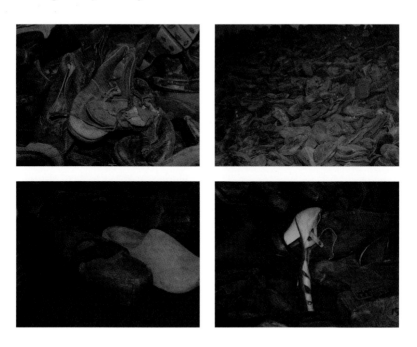

Third was the gas chamber. The hardest part of the tour was actually going into the gas chamber, which of course I had never done before. They used to cram nearly two thousand people in there, close the doors, and drop Zyklon B gas pellets through openings in the ceiling. This gas was heavy and settled near the floor at first; then it drifted up to the ceiling. This meant that everybody did not die at the same time. The young, the old, and the sick were always closest to the floor. People gasping for air climbed on top of other people and bodies, and the pile got higher and higher. Those closest to the floor died first. I cannot imagine what it was like for my mother being in there with her three grandchildren, Judy, Kathy, and Heddy. So many other members of my family perished there too—my brother Martin, his wife and their baby; my favourite grandfather, Jankev, my sister Regina. They all died in there … minutes … that's all they had.

I can still hear those voices as we waited on the platform in 1944: the crying, the praying, my mom's voice. Her last words to me were: "Better they should shoot you than touch you." Then we were separated and I didn't have a chance to ask her what she meant. But I recall overhearing my father talking with my mother at home and telling her that thousands of young women had been taken

83

from Austria and Czechoslovakia and trucked to the front lines to be used by the soldiers. When the troops moved on, the women were murdered and left in the fields. Perhaps that explains my mother's last words to me.

When I was eight or ten years old, my mother would read to us from the *Book of Esther* as we sat in a circle on the floor. This *Book* deals with an event that took place after the Persians had destroyed Babylon and Jews had been living for 210 years in captivity. The Persian king, Ahasuerus, gave Haman, the prime minister of Persia, total power and everyone was ordered to bow down before him whenever he passed. Mordecai, a Jewish man who had saved the Persian king's life earlier, refused to bow down before Haman, saying he only bowed down before his God. This angered Haman and he decided to kill all the Jews in the Persian Empire. Esther, the wife of Ahasuerus, was a Jewess, but the king didn't know this. She risked her life by telling the king about Haman's plot and saved her people from destruction. A two-day feast called Purim still celebrates the deliverance of the Jews to this day.

As a child I never understood why my mother would cry as she read this story to us. When I was 19, after being in Auschwitz for a few days and realizing that most of the people who were arriving there were being put to death immediately, I realized that my mother's worst fears were coming true. Another Haman had arisen. Then I knew why she had cried so much reading from the *Book of Esther*. And I understood why, in the boxcar on the way to Auschwitz-Birkenau, she had said she envied Sarah because she had had a proper burial. It was as if my mom knew what lay ahead for the rest of the family.

There had always been a strong bond between my mom and me. In spite of our different views of how much religion should control our lives, she was a very devoted person and I always felt close to her. I know she suffered a lot of pain with headaches and high blood pressure caused by major surgery she had after giving birth to my youngest sister, Fradel. Even as a young child I seemed to have a natural empathy for pain and suffering.

When I heard my mom using the old Singer sewing machine at 5:30 in the morning, I'd get out of bed and stand behind her and push the pedal as she sewed. It's no wonder I still wake up at that time. When she made bread on Monday and Friday mornings ... huge loaves, I mean, using 10 to 15 kilos of flour ... I would get up, put my hands in and help her knead the dough. She would tell me, "Keep doing it until your hands are clean."

My mother taught me a lot of things—how to be resourceful, how to be a good homemaker, how to cook and bake. I used to stand beside her, watching as she sewed beautiful tablecloths, one for each of the children, large enough to cover a table set for twelve. She also made other needlework items for our trousseaux, very delicate work known as Madeira or eyelets, that were different-shaped holes she cut out with tiny scissors. In the wintertime she saved all the duck and geese feathers that the family and neighbours gathered and separated the down from the rest of the feather. This down was used to make pillows and comforters for our trousseaux as well. All of this was left behind—lost forever—when we were taken to Auschwitz-Birkenau.

Even after sixty-three years, I still have difficulty dealing with those feelings.

Once we were out of the boxcars, they separated the women from the men and the selection was made by people like Dr. Joseph Mengele, the "Angel of Death." They decided who would live to become slave labourers and who would be sent straight to the gas chambers. I survived the selection thanks

to two unrelated events. First, when we had arrived at the camp, one of the prisoners persuaded me to give my niece Judy to my mom. Women with children were sent directly to the gas chambers. Second, when we were told to take our clothes off, I draped mine over my arm, unintentionally hiding the scar from my recent appendectomy.

Any "flaw" made a person unacceptable for slave labour, and they went to the gas chambers as well. My brother Martin had been born with one leg shorter than the other. Without his special shoes, he had a noticeable limp when he walked. He was sent to the gas chambers as soon as this was noticed.

After the selection we were put in barrack 11, which had a capital A over the doorway. Supposedly this was one of the better barracks. I didn't realize till later that the A stood for *Arbeit*, which means "work" in German. We were put in that section because we were going to be taken away later to work as slave labourers. Records found at Auschwitz show that 405,000 prisoners were selected as labourers between 1940 and 1945. Of these about 340,000 perished through executions, beatings, starvation, and sickness.

My sister and I and six other prisoners ended up on the top "bunk." It was more square than long, and there was no straw,

no mattress, nothing. There wasn't enough room for us to stretch our legs out, so we sat opposite each other, day and night, four on each side, our knees against our chests. You couldn't turn onto one side or the other. If you fell asleep, you fell asleep sitting. It was never any better than that for us.

In 1944, Hans Frank, the Governor General of Nazi-occupied Poland, said, "Jews are a race that must be totally exterminated." What makes it especially disturbing to me is that I know they wanted to kill me, but why did they torture us as they did?" I have a difficult time with that. One of the signs on our tour read: "Prisoners held in the concentration camp died from overwork,

starvation, sadistic punishments, exhaustion after prolonged roll calls, torture, appalling living conditions, being used for medical experiments, or arbitrary execution. Those too weak or sick to work were picked out by the SS during roll calls or in the infirmary and sent to the gas chambers or murdered with phenol injections." In the basement of one of the buildings, there were "standing cells," where four people were crammed into a small space, standing up, every night, after they had worked all day. Most of them died of exhaustion or suffocation, some after only a few days.

After the war, Rudolf Höss, the first commandant of Auschwitz, was tried for murder, sentenced to death, and hanged in Auschwitz I on April 16, 1947. He had organized and streamlined the techniques of mass murder at Auschwitz-Birkenau and was the first to use Zyklon B gas to kill victims. His wife and family lived in a house on the grounds of the camp. In the morning, he used to go and look through a peephole into the gas chamber to watch the people in there dying. Then he would return home to have his breakfast with his family.

I remember going out of the barrack and around to this long building to go to the toilet, having dysentery and no toilet paper. The smell just blew you away. The toilets were nothing but holes in a concrete structure set above the ground. You really wanted to get out of there as quickly as possible; it was that eerie to be in there. No wonder typhoid spread as quickly as it did. As many as 6,000 men and women lined up to use the same latrines. There was no pit below the latrine; it was only as deep as the height of the concrete structure. The prisoners had to clean them out when they were full.

I had a feeling that this woman was mourning, either someone close to her or just because she was touched by what she had seen.

When I saw the man and boy carrying flowers and walking down the track toward the memorial, I wondered what their connection was to this camp. Like me, they probably had relatives who were murdered there. When I walked along the tracks myself, all I could think about was my family .... how they walked ... . Within an hour—within one hour of their arrival—they were murdered. Within one hour seventy-five percent of those who arrived were gassed.

And there I was 63 years later, walking along, feeling free. Not free from the pain, because I still have to deal with it every day. Even now I have a hard time accepting and dealing with what happened there. It's still so hard to believe it really happened—over a million people killed in such a short time. The Nazis came close to fulfilling their goal of exterminating all the Jews of Europe.

The SS tried to destroy Krema II and III, the crematoria, as the Soviet troops advanced toward the camp, but enough was left behind for everyone to see what they had been doing. There was more destruction in Birkenau because that's where the murdering went on, and they wanted to get rid of the evidence before the Russians arrived.

The memorial at Birkenau looked like figures … bodies … an oven … a wall. Perhaps it was meant to represent a camp, because it had gates, and pits. The large black blocks seem to have fallen over, but that's part of the sculpture. Maybe they represent all the "fallen" people who died so close to that place.

It was very bleak, very dark, but I can understand why. I placed a stone there in memory of my family.

Two of the warehouses were called Canada I and II—*Kanada* in German—because Canada was thought to be a land of plenty and opportunity. These warehouses had the best items that were confiscated from the Jews as they arrived on the trains, including fur coats, diamonds, pots and pans, and canned food. My family didn't have what some people had.

I never had a toothbrush until I got to Sweden. At home there was always some baking soda in a little dish and you dipped your finger in it and rubbed your teeth.

Memories of my mother are stronger now because I had the opportunity to walk around, go into the gas chamber, sit and think, whereas in 1944 it all happened so suddenly. There was so much more going on at Auschwitz-Birkenau than I had realized when I was there before. On September 28, 2007, I had the opportunity to look at things from the outside, knowing what was going on. It's like when you are in a room in a huge building. You know what's going on in that room and that building, but if you don't get out of that room or building, you don't know what's happening in the next building or the next room.

This time, I saw things I was not aware of when I was there before. At that time I lived in just one barrack, and going to the kitchen to get the soup was as far as I went. You didn't go from one section of Auschwitz-Birkenau to another section unless you were taken for a reason, and they certainly didn't show you those horrible places. You didn't hear about everything that was happening in the camps. Who was going to tell you? That's why you came away from there so overwhelmed. I saw enough, but Birkenau was a huge, huge killing machine, and I had no way of knowing what was going on in the next section of the camp or in Block 11, where they tortured people. I had never seen those little cubicles in Auschwitz I, where prisoners were forced people to stand until they died.

At the end of our visit to Auschwitz-Birkenau I was absolutely devastated. I couldn't have imagined that after 63 years being there would have such an effect on me. It was overwhelming, even though so much of the camp has been torn down. Seeing the gas chamber … thinking about my mom and my nieces ... the shoes, especially the children's shoes … I had not been that sad in a very long time. It was overwhelming to make such a journey at age 82, to walk the tracks, to walk the ground where I was once imprisoned. I didn't know how I was going to put it into the right perspective, or if it was even possible to do that. Time will tell what I will be able to do with it. Right then I felt hollow, empty; everything was gone.

There is where hope lies, to see young people come and visit the camps. When I get home and go out to speak, I want the students in Canada to see pictures of me in the camps and realize what commitment means.

When I saw the destruction I realized even more the value of compassion and love.

6

BUCHENWALD

Tolerance should only be a temporary attitude.
It must lead to recognition. To tolerate means to offend.

Goethe quote on the cafeteria wall at Buchenwald

Tolerance isn't good enough. It means someone

still thinks there's something "wrong" with you.

That may only mean that they won't kill you. But

what does it really mean if they don't respect you?

Eva Olsson

Ettersberg is a 1478-metre-high hill overlooking peaceful farming country 10 kilometres northwest of Weimar, several hours west of Berlin. Goethe, the German novelist, poet, playwright, and scientist used to climb the Ettersberg to sit and work under a large oak tree that sat in the midst of a beech forest. In July 1937, the Nazis began to construct a concentration camp there and chose to call it Buchenwald ("beech forest") because of the close ties of the location to Goethe, who was being idealized as "the embodiment of the German spirit." A photo taken in 1944 shows that the Goethe oak had been left inside the camp. All that remains now is the stump and a plaque.

Häftlingswäscherei und „Goethe-Eiche", Foto Juni 1944
insgeheim von dem französischen Häftling Georges Angeli aufgenommen
Inmates' laundry and "Goethe Oak," photograph, june 1944
photo taken secretly by the French inmate Georges Angeli
Buanderie des détenus et „Chêne de Goethe", juin 1944
photo prise clandestinement par le détenu français Georges Angeli
Прачечная для узников и „Дуб Гёте", фотоснимок июнь 1944 г.
втайне снят французким узником Георгес Ангели

12

Buchenwald was not an "extermination camp" like Auschwitz-Birkenau; it and its subcamps were important sources of slave labour for nearby armaments factories, stone quarries, and construction projects. Its goal was the destruction of the prisoners by work, torture, beatings, starvation, and lack of hygiene. Between July 1937 and April 1945, 250,000 people from all over Europe were imprisoned there. Of these, approximately 56,000—including 11,000 Jews—died in the camp.

The sign overhead at the entrance to Buchenwald cynically reads Jedem das seine—*"To each his own" or "Everybody gets what he deserves."*

In July of 1937, the first 149 inmates arrived at the camp, mostly members of the resistance, political prisoners, Jehovah's Witnesses, previously convicted criminals, and a few homosexuals. They were put to work clearing the forest, laying sewer pipes and power lines, building roads, houses, garages, and a barrack camp.

In November, 1938, in the aftermath of Kristallnacht, German SS and police sent nearly 10,000 Jews to Buchenwald.

On September 27, 1939, a special camp surrounded by barbed wire was set up on the muster ground in the centre of the camp. Among its first inmates were 110 Poles, who died of hunger and cold within a few weeks. In October, over 3,000 Poles and Jews were crowded into tents in this special camp and killed by intentional starvation, terror, and neglect.

In September, 1941, the first Soviet prisoners arrived there, and over the next two years, the SS Commando Unit 99 killed over 8,500 of them by shooting them in the neck as they lined up against a wall to have their height measured. Loud music was played to cover the sounds of the killings.

In 1941, a program of involuntary medical experiments on prisoners began in special barracks in the northern part of the main camp. Medical experiments involving viruses and contagious diseases such as typhus resulted in hundreds of deaths. In 1944, SS Dr. Carl Vaernet began a series of experiments that he claimed would "cure" homosexual inmates.

On April 11, 1945, as American forces were advancing on Buchenwald, most of the SS guards fled. The starved and emaciated prisoners stormed the watchtowers and seized control of the camp. Later that afternoon, the American forces entered the camp.

On April 16, 1945, the American Army commander ordered that one thousand citizens of Weimar be brought to Buchenwald to tour the camp and see the death and horror their government had been perpetrating in their name 10 kilometres away from their homes.

Photographer Margaret Bourke-White was with the troops when they entered the camp, and photographed the horrific scene for Life Magazine. *She recalls:*

> *We didn't know! We didn't know! I first heard these words on a sunny afternoon in mid-April, 1945. They were repeated so often in the weeks to come, and all of us heard them with such monotonous frequency, that we came to regard them as a kind of national chant for Germany.*

Buchenwald was one of the toughest days of the trip for all of us, and we were surprised at how we felt. I'm not sure why that happened. Perhaps we underestimated what we were going to experience at the camp, because we'd been told "there isn't much to see there." I think part of the reason we were all so affected by Buchenwald is the fact that we were still processing emotions from our visit to Auschwitz-Birkenau two days earlier. We—especially Eva—had worked hard to stay in control at Auschwitz-Birkenau. Maybe we let our guard down when we went to Buchenwald and were overwhelmed by how awful it was.

We left Krakow on September 29 at 7:55 AM and arrived in Weimar at 9 PM. Having a whole day on the train worked out very well after our very stressful train trip from Satu Mare to Krakow and the day spent at Auschwitz-Birkenau. It gave us a chance to spend some quiet time reflecting on what we had seen and heard at the concentration camp that day.

Another of the amazing "coincidences" of the trip happened during that journey. As I took notes, Eva and I talked for over an hour about Satu Mare and Auschwitz-Birkenau. A few minutes after I put away my notebook, the man sitting behind us leaned over the back of the seat and said, "Please excuse me for eavesdropping, but I am sitting here listening to you talk and crying. You're talking about Satu Mare, where my ancestors come from." And thus we met Simon Srebrny, a British journalist who is living in Berlin and working for

Deutsche Welle, a television network. He was returning from two weeks researching his family history, and couldn't believe his ears when he heard Eva and me talking about Satu Mare. Many of his relatives had perished in Auschwitz-Birkenau, so he was very interested in talking to Eva.

We chatted with Simon for the next few hours. I showed him the old pictures of Jews in Sighet that Johnny Popescu had downloaded from his computer onto my memory stick, and he gasped as he recognized some of his ancestors, including Rabbi Teitelbaum. He copied the pictures to his computer.

When we arrived in Berlin, he gave Eva a long, tearful hug before we parted.

We had over an hour before we had to catch the train to Weimar, so we decided to grab a bite to eat in the station. That was a good move, as there were dozens of places to buy food— from coffee shops to gourmet restaurants—selling a wide variety of German and international specialties. The hardest part was making the choice of what to buy. Yvonne solved this problem when she returned with a plate of fresh fish and chips that looked so good we all ended up buying that too. All washed down with, of course, a mug of German beer.

The new five-level Berlin Hauptbahnhof opened in 2006, after 10 years of construction and $850 million, and it's absolutely dazzling. Being just a short distance from Government buildings, the Brandenburg Gate, Potsdamer Platz, and the Holocaust Memorial, it has become one of Berlin's key tourist attractions.

The station was full of people, understandable considering that there are 15,000 square metres of retail space on three levels. In addition, every day 1850 long-distance, regional, and rapid transit trains stop at the 14 platforms on two different levels, with trains leaving the station in all directions every 90 seconds. It was quite a sensory rush after the sombre day at Auschwitz-Birkenau and the relative calm of the day on the train. As I went down an escalator to find the information board, I could see and hear trains coming and going both above and below me, very much like the futuristic cities in *Star Wars* and other science fiction movies.

The station was designed to be a symbol of the newly reunited Germany at the centre of an ever-more integrated Europe. On the upper level, east-west trains on three platforms link Moscow and Paris, crossing eight tracks and four platforms two levels below, where north-south trains connect Copenhagen and Istanbul. Two glass towers are connected by a bridge with a glass roof soaring 150 feet above the main platforms, sending shafts of light throughout the station below. Fifty-four escalators and 43 round glass-enclosed elevators mean there's motion in every direction you look—dazzling and dizzying at the same time. There are solar cells on the glass ceiling, raised strips on the platforms to guide the blind, and acoustical features to muffle the racket of passing trains.

We were on the platform for our train to Weimar with time to spare, and the high-speed train arrived right on time. The only problem was that our car was at the front of the train and ended up about as far away from us as possible, causing us to have to run the length of the platform to leap on board before it flew out of the station. Later I recalled that most European stations have an information board showing exactly where each car will stop. The trip from Berlin to Weimar took two and a half hours, and we arrived at nine o'clock Saturday evening.

Before the Nazi takeover of power, Weimar was a major cultural centre, home at times to Schiller, Franz Liszt, and Bach, as well as Goethe, who embodied the German enlightenment of the eighteenth century. In 1919 it was the birthplace of German constitutional democracy, the Weimar Republic, as well as the Bauhaus school of art, design, and architecture. The contrast between the liberal humanism of the elegant Weimar and the brutality of the desolate Buchenwald makes it hard to believe that the same nation produced both of them.

The next morning we boarded a local bus across the square from our hotel and made the 25-minute journey to Buchenwald. When we got on the bus, there were no empty seats. Most of the seats were taken by young people, who were chatting and playing with their cell phones and iPods. None of them offered Eva their seat, in marked contrast to Hungary and Romania, where young people had jumped up immediately when we boarded a bus or streetcar. After five minutes or so, a middle-aged man gave Eva his seat.

The countryside between Weimar and Buchenwald was lush and green, everything perfectly maintained and serene. The shortness of the trip and the laughing, exuberant young people may have heightened the impact of the concentration camp. We rented a self-guided-tour tape player and set out to explore the camp.

There was a very moving exhibition of art in the former disinfection building. Many of the pieces featured shoes or a suitcase.

The only reason I wanted to go to Buchenwald was because my father died of starvation there in December 1944. When I had inquired years before, I got a letter from the authorities in Weimar saying that they couldn't find any record of my father in Buchenwald. However, I learned from a man who been a neighbor in Satu Mare that my father had died there, only seven months after we were shipped in boxcars from Satu Mare on May 15. It's hard for me to comprehend such a healthy man dying within seven months. He'd never been sick; he wasn't old. However, I have read that prisoners in many of the camps who couldn't find extra food beyond what they were given died of starvation after several months.

I was hoping to see the records at Buchenwald, but that wasn't possible. I wanted to see if any other relatives were imprisoned or died there, perhaps some of my mother's cousins. The Nazis kept careful track of every detail so they could prove to the world that they had killed all the Jews. They were very proud of what they were accomplishing. But as the Allied troops were closing in on the camps and Germany was about to lose the war, the Nazis probably realized the rest of the world might not think so highly of their activities, so they destroyed a lot of the records to cover up what they had been doing.

Although I have searched, I don't know where my brother Lazar died. Remembrance Day is different for me than for many people. I don't know where the wind has blown my brother's ashes so I can't go anywhere to place a wreath.

Pol	33150	Matylewicz Wladislaus	geb	4.6.97
·	33151	Mitschke Heinrich	·	13.6.91
⊕	33153	Mroz Thadeus	·	5.11.05
·	33154	Mussil Roman	·	8.1.20
·	33155	Muszynski Thadeus	·	29.9.89
·	33156	Nadachowski Kasimir	·	17.8.69
·	33157	Ottmann Wladimir	·	26.11.76
·	33158	Palczewski Thadeus	·	3.12.14
·	33159	Pomkiewicz Adam	·	29.9.11
·	33160	Pazdzierny Stanislaus	·	14.4.95
·	33161	Petrinski Borys	·	27.11.91
·	33162	Pobudkiewicz Marian	·	21.10.06
⊘	33164	Puget Ludwig	·	21.6.77
·	33165	Pykosz Zbigniew	"	23.4.12
⊘	33166	Rozycki Thadeus	"	15.3.08
·	33167	Romanowicz Thadeus	"	27.5.17
⊘	33168	Rubczak Johann	·	18.1.82
·	33169	Sadkowski Kasimir	"	24.6.86
⊘	33171	Siwek Karl	"	15.3.10
·	33172	Skwara Siegmund	·	13.1.19
·	33173	Sleczek Thadeus	"	29.3.18
·	33174	Sliwinski Adam	"	22.12.89
✗	33175	Sliwinski Adam	"	13.12.17
·	33176	Sochacki Roman	"	25.4.98
·	33177	Stande Georg	"	12.10.16
✗	33178	Stefanowicz Georg	·	8.3.80
·	33180	Szyla Wladislaus	"	9.2.00
·	33181	Szarota Stefan		10.11.11

25 14617

Although I am alone, he is with me in spirit and I will always love him.

I wanted to see if I could find some peace and put together more pieces of the puzzle from my childhood. But I have not been able to do that. I came away from Buchenwald with a lot less than I had hoped for. There was no peace between me and my father in the last few years of his life, and I hoped going there would be a kind of closure. But now, many months later, I see that hasn't happened. Did I find peace there? No. But I'm dealing with that. This is something I'll just have to put to sleep, even though it's not a closed chapter for me.

Most of all I just wanted to walk on the ground my father last walked on, and I did that. I hope he knows I was there.

When we returned to the hotel in Weimar that day, Ron asked me if I had been able to say goodbye to my father, and I said yes. But that doesn't mean I have forgotten him or the difficulties we had with each other. I guess I was hoping that I'd be able to let it go, but I have to accept the fact that it will never be over between us. Have I forgiven him? Oh, definitely. I had to release him, to release his soul so he can rest in peace. I'm not angry and I don't hold any malice toward him. No human being on earth deserves to die the way he did.

My father and I didn't get along because as a teenager I had great difficulty dealing with the fundamentalist way of life his Hasidic religion demanded. We were not allowed to look out the window because a boy might go by and see us. I wasn't allowed to go to school, and that has bothered me all of my life. It's only in recent years that I have accepted the fact that I was different. I haven't figured that out why I was different. It's probably genetic, not necessarily from my parents. At a very young age I rebelled against this restrictive upbringing, and my parents were aware of it. I know I caused my father a lot of stress. And the reverse is also true.

When I was standing by the tracks he would have arrived on at Buchenwald, I was looking hard inside myself. But I could only see and hear my father as I remembered him from my childhood, and I couldn't find any peace or any love. I still don't understand why I never loved my dad. Never. And that still bothers me. Why did I always fear my dad, even as a young child? I never feared my mother or my grandfather. Did I see something in him that I can't remember? If I could remember, then I might be able to deal with it: "Oh right, this is why I didn't love my dad." He didn't start punishing me until I was around eight years of age, and then it was frequent. I was out of control, according to his religious beliefs. Did he see me as a bad child? Probably, but other children can love their parents even if they're seen as bad.

My sister Fradel said that my younger brother Lazar had followed in my footsteps, and was not a very good child. Well, my father probably thought that I wasn't a good child either. But even though children are sometimes made to feel they are not good, they still usually love their fathers. But I didn't.

My father disciplined Lazar the same way as he did me. One evening Lazar decided not to go to prayers, and went to a movie instead. When my father asked him where he had been, Lazar said he had gone to the other synagogue. When my father checked with people there and found out that wasn't true, he came home and started to hit Lazar. I can still see Lazar, who was a big, tall boy, slamming his fists on the kitchen table saying, "The more you hit me, the more I will go to the movies." Now this is a good example of what I'm saying about discipline. If the evening prayers were so important to my father, why didn't he say to his son, "Go to the early prayers and then go to the movie."

When I was a small child, I didn't have of a lot of contact with my father, so maybe it's not all that unnatural that I didn't love him. In the early years he was around, but later, while he was writing his books, he was away a lot. When he would come home, he wouldn't hug us, but he would kiss us on the head. He wouldn't touch the girls after we were 12, because we might be having our period, and that would make us "unclean." I used to like to go to the printing place with my father because I was fascinated with the typesetting. Other than that, none of us did anything with our father. I think about how tragic it is that a man who was clever, a teacher who wrote 18 religious books, could discipline the two of us so harshly because of his religious beliefs. As a child I just went to bed at night, did my crying there, and I was okay in the morning. I didn't hate him for what he did. I was saddened by it.

On the other hand, I was around my mother a lot and helped her do things, so I knew her well. I knew her moods and what she liked and didn't like. My bond with my mother started before I was born. The doctors didn't want her to have me, so she stayed in bed for the whole pregnancy. We had a special bond, and she always used to tell me I was the best child she had. Actually, I always enjoyed helping her.

My youngest sister, Fradel, was the only one of the children who had a different bond with our father, because he used to put her to bed every night. She slept in the same room as my parents, and the other five kids slept in the other room. When we lived at 36 Petofi Street and Fradel didn't want to go to bed, my father would pick her up and put her in his bed. He would lie beside her until she had fallen asleep, then he would carry her to my mom's bed.

My other sisters, Sarah and Regina, never disagreed with my father or argued with him; they obeyed him just like sweet lambs. Whenever Regina would say she didn't want to run an errand because it was raining or snowing, I would volunteer to go, because I wanted to be out of the house.

When I was 18, I was sent on a seven-hour journey to Debrecen on an errand for my parents. While I was there, I went to see a movie for the first time in my life. My father must have had people there following me and spying on me, because he found out. He took me into the courtyard outside our house and beat and kicked me over and over. I have tried very hard to understand how he could punish me the way he did. I wonder if he hated me. I cannot let go of that, even though I never hated him.

Where did my father's anger come from? That day my father went way beyond anger to rage. He was practically frothing at the mouth as he beat me. If my mom had not opened the door and said, "Haim Ytzhog, that is enough," how far would he have taken it? Would I still be here had my mom not opened the door? I still think about that. My father was kicking me in the hip with his boots. If I had been permanently damaged and had a limp, I might not have survived the selection at Auschwitz-Birkenau and would have gone straight to the gas chamber. One of my brother Martin's legs was a bit shorter than the other, causing him to limp when he wasn't wearing his special shoes. When they saw this, they sent him straight to the gas chamber.

That beating cut whatever emotional ties there were between me and my father. I think that beating did me in or did him in, or both. The only time I spoke to him in the next year and a half was when he told me he wanted to marry me to a young man in his yeshiva. I knew this man because he would eat at our house once a week. I said to my father, "If you force me to marry him, I will run away." He said nothing. When I went in to the kitchen, my mom said that I should accept my father's wishes. I told my mom that it was Yidu, my aunt Sarah's [mom's sister] stepson, that I wanted to marry. He was in the army and when he was away, he used to write to me and send the letters to the neighbours across the street who had the grocery store. My mother said she knew her sister's stepchildren were good people, but she wondered what kind of clothes our children would wear, since Yidu wore modern clothes, not the black Hasidic ones. She was only concerned about what it would look like to others. After a while, the letters stopped coming. Yidu had died in the Ukraine, and that ended that.

That's the last time I spoke to my father, except when I was spoken to or to answer a question. I could not continue speaking to someone who had so much anger inside himself and who took it out on his children. That was still true two years later when we took Sarah to Budapest.

Shortly after we got back to Canada, I was really upset when I heard about Muhammed Parvez, the man in Mississauga who was charged with strangling his 16-year-old daughter, Aqsa, while they were arguing. I guess I was especially sensitive to this story because my memories of the time my father beat me so viciously had been stirred up at Buchenwald. I found it easy to imagine myself in her shoes. However, unlike the young girl, I was lucky because my mother stepped in to help me. While I was damaged emotionally, at least I wasn't killed.

Some early reports in the news said that the girl was murdered by her father because she didn't want to wear the head scarf [hijab]. Other reports said she wanted to dress and act more like the other girls, and this went against her father's religious beliefs. Some people said he feared losing control of his daughter and looking bad in his religious community. Right now we don't know what caused the disagreement, but the father has been charged with strangling his daughter, and the young girl is dead. That should never have happened.

If it was because of his religious beliefs, it's a tragedy. But we can't just blame religion for what people do. People make decisions and must accept responsibility for them. If it turns out that the father did strangle his daughter, there's a lesson there for other parents who don't want to make the same mistake: Don't discipline when you're angry.

Children do need discipline and guidance from adults, but we cannot teach children with anger. It doesn't work. I'm a prime example of that. I used to get spanked a lot, and it didn't change my behaviour. What might have worked is discipline with love and compassion. Children can understand and accept that, but they rebel against harsh, severe discipline. Had my father been able to discipline me and my brother Lazar in a compassionate way, through dialogue, sitting down, talking, and explaining, the result might have been different. In my presentation, I ask parents to discipline their children with love, for the benefit of the child, not the parent, and for the right reasons.

When I talk to kids at schools, they tell me that discipline with anger just backfires. I have a letter from a grade six student telling me he became a bully because his parents are always yelling at him when he doesn't do what his parents want him to do. They shout: "You left your boots in the hallway!" instead of saying, "I really don't like your leaving your boots there. Could you please put them over there?" The problem is the same, but the result is different.

We need to be more careful how and why we discipline. I wasn't disciplined for my benefit. I was disciplined because my father was disappointed that he could not control me. Lazar told me that he had overheard my parents talking, and my father was bothered by the fact that I had just accepted his punishment and not talked back to him.

What religion says that you can't be a good human being because you go to a movie or you want be like your classmates? It's a tragedy when we say to our children, "You have to do this or that," in the name of our religion. When the child gets older, he will choose his own religious path. So I can't agree with forcing children to follow their parents' religious beliefs. When children grow up in an environment where there's a lot of hate, that's what they take with them.

I almost ended up at Buchenwald in February 1945. By that time my father would already have been dead for two months. We were being shipped from the Krupp plant as the Allied armies were advancing, and we had no idea where we were going. The train ride was horrific, because the train went backward and forward, shunting from one track to another to avoid the bombing that was in progress. We were on the train for quite a few days without food. At night the train would sit still because the bombs were dropping all around us and they couldn't move.

One day we stopped at a camp, which I believed was Buchenwald. I saw electrical fences, prisoners who looked like skeletons walking around, dead bodies on the ground, and male prisoners wearing odd caps who stared at the train. The SS left our train

and entered the camp. The fear of them taking us off this train and putting us in this camp was almost unbearable. When the SS returned to the train we continued our journey. Later that evening a Hungarian guard told us they wouldn't take us in that camp because it was overcrowded. I thought it was a miracle that we weren't let into that camp, even though we didn't know where we were going to end up. I now know that the camp we stopped at was Buchenwald, because Ron found this account in a journal on the Internet:

More than five hundred Hungarian women had been indentured as slave labour in the Krupp munitions works in nearby Essen. Their heads shaven, garbed in burlap sacks, housed in unheated barracks through the winter, set upon by dogs to prod them in their work, they had performed like robots until the intensive Allied bombardment began. They were forbidden access to the air-raid shelters and huddled together in terror in open trenches. The plants destroyed, Krupp officials herded the survivors into freight cars and sent them to Buchenwald, for the girls had been merely 'on loan.' The German camp commandant could not accept them since he had already received thousands of other prisoners from camps also under fire. The girls were not even unloaded for bodily relief before being shipped on to dreaded Bergen-Belsen.

The Jewish memorial at Buchenwald is very different from the memorial at Auschwitz-Birkenau, which had tall columns and steps. This memorial is a pit full of rocks brought from

the nearby quarry, in memory of the Jews who were forced to work there. It's very dark and desolate, with no hope.

All those who died there—whether they were the Roma people (gypsies), Jehovah's Witnesses, Russian prisoners of war, homosexuals, political prisoners, or disabled people—died for no good reason, no just cause. They died because of someone else's hate.

Again it struck me that when people were told to pack, some of them chose fancy dress shoes. This makes it more sad to me and reinforced the notion of how cynical the German SS were. The woman who chose these white shoes thought she was going on a journey, to be "resettled" somewhere else.

People were given two hours to pack what they could carry. They were told to bring "important" things.

Another way to kill prisoners was used in the stable. The prisoners had to enter a fake infirmary room and place themselves under a height gauge. At this time, an SS man killed them with a revolver by shooting through a small hole placed at the height of the prisoner's neck. The noise of those executions was masked by a radio at maximum volume.

The boy in the picture survived because he was hidden for four years by the adult prisoners. He is shown enjoying his first walk outdoors on the day the camp was liberated.

I don't know how children could survive in the camps, but 904 survived at Buchenwald. This is a well-known story told by one of them:

Israel's former Chief Rabbi, Yisrael Meir Lau, was one of hundreds of children held prisoner at Buchenwald. He recalled the moment when American soldiers arrived and Rabbi Herschel Schachter, the Jewish chaplain of the division, embraced him.

"He came in and met me, a child of less than 8 years old. He took me in his arms, weeping and trying to smile and laugh," Rabbi Lau said. "Holding me in his arms, he asked me, 'How old are you, my child?' "What difference does it make?" I answered, warily. "I'm older than you, anyway."

'Why do you think you are older?' he asked me. I said, "Because you laugh and cry like a child. I don't cry, and I haven't laughed for a long time. So which one of us is older?"

Buchenwald

7

BERGEN-BELSEN

The memory of the apocalyptic epoch of the Holocaust should become part of the human conscience and consciousness for all time. Beyond sorrow, suffering, and death, the tragic annihilation of European Jewry must inspire humankind to commit itself against all manifestations of genocide and racial hatred. May a new love for humanity be born out of the horrors we have known.

from the Scroll of Remembrance
at Bergen-Belsen

Bergen-Belsen concentration camp was located 60 kilometres northeast of Hannover, Germany, on the Lüneburg Heath, near the town of Celle. In 1940 it was set up as a prisoner of war camp, and between then and 1942, 18,000 Soviet prisoners died there of disease, cold, and hunger. In 1942 it became a concentration camp for Jews, Gypsies, homosexuals, and political dissidents and was handed over to the SS in April 1943. The "Star Camp" was a part of the camp set aside to hold several thousand Jews who were to be exchanged for money or for German civilians interned in various countries overseas. Only 358 of the Jews at Bergen-Belsen obtained their freedom through an exchange for other prisoners.

In 1945 larger numbers of prisoners arrived at the camp from other camps as the Russians advanced from the east. The number of inmates increased from 22,000 on February 1, to 41,520 on March 1, and ultimately to about 60,000 on April 15, when the camp was liberated. These numbers completely overwhelmed the camp's facilities and led to the spread of disease. There were no gas chambers at this camp, but over 50,000 people died there, including 35,000 people who died in the three-month period from February to April 1945, mostly from starvation, dehydration, and rampant diseases such as typhus. The small crematorium couldn't keep up with the rate of death. The nearby German Army garrison had facilities for baking 60,000 loaves of bread daily, but they had been providing only 10,000 loaves per day to the concentration camp, while keeping the rest to feed the German soldiers.

British forces (including some Canadians) entered the camp on April 15, 1945 and were horrified at what they saw: over 10,000 unburied, naked bodies, and thousands of walking skeletons. The stench of the rotting corpses was so great that British soldiers said they could smell the camp 10 miles away. They were so worried about the possibility that disease would spread from the piles of bodies that they dug large pits to be used as mass graves for up to 5,000 bodies at a time. At first, they made the SS guards carry bodies to the pits, but eventually they resorted to pushing the bodies in with bulldozers.

Nearly 14,000 people died after the camp was liberated, because they were so ill that their bodies couldn't respond to the food and medicine. After moving all the surviving prisoners to a nearby German army camp, the British burned everything in the original camp on May 21, 1945. The army base became a Displaced Persons camp until 1950, populated largely by Jews waited to get into Palestine or some other country. Most Jews did not want to return to Poland or other Eastern European countries because their former Jewish communities no longer existed, but anti-Semitism did.

German civilians from the towns of Bergen and Belsen were brought to tour the camp on April 25, 1945, and a British officer made the following comments to them:

What you will see here is the final and utter condemnation of the Nazi party. It justifies every measure the United Nations will take to exterminate that party. What you will see here is such a disgrace to the German people that their names must be erased from the list of civilized nations ... It is your lot to begin the hard task of restoring the name of the German people ... But this cannot be done until you have reared a new generation amongst whom it is impossible to find people prepared to commit such crimes; until you have reared a new generation possessing the instinctive good will to prevent a repetition of such horrible cruelties.

Today, the Memorial Site sits on only a small portion of the former Bergen-Belsen concentration camp. All that remains now is a large park-like field, several monuments, and the heather-covered mounds over the burial pits that contain over 50,000 bodies. There is a documentation centre where the history of the camp and its victims are displayed, and a new museum that opened at the end of October 2007. A film shown in several languages documents the horrific scene the British forces found when they entered the camp.

The English translation of the inscription on the Jewish Monument reads:

Israel and the world shall remember thirty thousand Jews exterminated in the concentration camp of Bergen-Belsen at the hands of the murderous Nazis.

EARTH CONCEAL NOT THE BLOOD SHED ON THEE!

The train trip from Weimar to Hannover took three hours, and we arrived at noon. It was too late to make the two-hour trip to Bergen-Belsen, so Yvonne and Don took a tour of the city, following a route marked on the sidewalk. Eva and I relaxed at the hotel and then took a walk, stopping at a travel agent to book our tickets on the ferry from Lübeck to Sweden in two days.

We took a train the next day to a small town called Celle, and then a taxi to the concentration camp. Our taxi driver lived in Celle and said he had taken many people to the camp over the years, but he had never gone inside. Maybe he didn't want to know what happened there; perhaps he just didn't want to see. After the others had gone ahead into the information centre and I was paying him, he asked me to "tell the lady how much I admire her courage." He told me that his own parents had lost everything at the end of the war when they fled from eastern Germany ahead of the Russian army.

Somewhat disconcertingly, the whole time we walked around the site of the former camp, we heard the sounds of war—tank fire coming from the NATO tank gunnery range next to the memorial site.

At the end of January 1945 we began to hear rumours that they were going to take us away from the Krupp slave factory. A Hungarian soldier who was part of the Nazi guards sometimes told us a bit about what was going on, and that was a help. Around the middle of February they did take us away in boxcars. As I mentioned in an earlier chapter, our train stopped at Buchenwald, but they were already overflowing, so we moved on. At the time we thought we were lucky not to have been put in that camp. How wrong we were.

When we arrived at Bergen-Belsen, the view just numbed us. I can still see that scene: death, sickness, and devastation everywhere. The ground was littered with dead bodies. There were literally hills of dead bodies, some of them as high as a man can reach. And the smell ... most of the prisoners had dysentery (non-stop diarrhea) and were lying in their own waste. In the barracks, there wasn't a chair to sit on, or a bunk, or a table ... nothing. Dead or alive, you were on the floor. The first person I saw was a neighbour's daughter, whose parents owned the grocery store across the street from us in Satu Mare. She was sitting on the floor, with a metal mug in her hands.

While most of the other prisoners had dysentery, I had the opposite problem. For ten days I couldn't go to the bathroom. The body needs food before it can produce waste, and we were barely getting starvation rations. Some people survived by eating grass and licking the dew off the grass. Other prisoners drank water from trenches that were contaminated with the human waste that ran out of the barracks.

At 4:30 every morning we were forced to stand outside for roll call, which lasted for two hours, sometimes longer. They never told us why. They just did it. The barrack was half full of dead people. Many others were skeletons who couldn't pull themselves outside. I can still see the SS woman sticking her head into the barracks, looking around, and counting those who were lying on the floor and couldn't go out to be counted. What was the purpose of that? Nazi efficiency. Keep track of everybody; make sure nobody runs away.

People had names, but the Nazis gave them numbers instead. They documented everything so that they could show the world they had done what they said they were going to do—eliminate all the Jews of Europe. You have to remember that the Nazis were very intelligent, educated murderers. They weren't just your everyday truck drivers or bricklayers. It seemed that the better educated they were the more cruel they were.

This went on for two and a half months, until we were liberated. I consider myself lucky that I wasn't there longer, because I likely would have died, as over 50,000 people did. When the British liberated the camp, they sent in 90 medical interns to help the sick. They couldn't find an inch of space in the barracks that was free of excrement where they could walk or lay the sick to treat them. Many prisoners were so ill and far gone that they were treated on the spot as best they could be. The British fed the prisoners only a clear broth, but almost 14,000 of them died in the six weeks after the liberation. Those who managed to live were later removed to tent areas as the barracks were burned to the ground to prevent the spread of disease. Fradel and I were lucky and were taken to the nearby hospital.

Just as I was getting better, my sister's condition worsened. Fradel caught typhus and was delirious with fever, talking in her sleep at night. She thought she was back at home. One time she said, "It's Friday. You have to go and clean the boys' shoes and get their white shirts out," because the girls usually got the boys' clothes ready for the Sabbath. She was not doing very well. I was getting better because I had already been quite sick before we were liberated.

I could not bear to see my sister so sick. One day a doctor came in, looked at me, looked at my sister, and started to leave without making a comment. I got out of bed and went after her. I said to her, "You can't let her die." The doctor kept going, so I grabbed her by her white coat and said, "You cannot let her die. She's all I have." The doctor said, "I'll see what I can do." She came back with a needle, gave my sister an injection, and said, "That's really all I can do for her. If it works, she will live, and if it doesn't work, she won't." My sister slept and slept and woke up two or three days later, feeling better. Obviously, that medication helped her, whatever it was. She got better and that helped me.

I didn't know what to expect, what we were going to see when we went back this time. I knew there were going to be mass graves, because that's how they dealt with the thousands of bodies they found when they liberated the camp. And it wasn't even a killing centre; they just took people there to die—no water, no food.

When we were entering the camp this time, I kept saying to myself: "Did I really come out of here?" When I was lying on the barrack floor in 1945, I said to myself, "I cannot die. I will not die here. They've already taken just about everything else away from me. But they can't kill the strength that's inside of me—my spirit." We started to get lice all over us, and it was impossible to get rid of them. I got sick about two weeks before we were liberated. I didn't know what I had then, but it was Fleck typhus ("spotted fever"), which is transmitted by lice and was rampant in the camp.

The plaques and grave markers really moved me. They don't mark real graves, but are symbolic. One that really affected me was placed there by three children who had survived the camp, in memory of their parents who had perished there.

There was a very modern building off to the side where you could go and sit quietly. Many people had left messages on a table at the front. Anne Frank and her older sister, Margot, died of typhus at Bergen-Belsen in March 1945, shortly before the liberation, so there were many pictures of her and a symbolic gravestone.

I remember when I was a young girl going with my mom in Satu Mare to visit her parents' graves, and she always placed a stone there. I never asked her where that tradition came from, but I have since read that Jews traditionally didn't place

flowers on graves but put stones there instead. The origin of that custom is uncertain but may relate to the fact that in ancient times a pile of stones was used as a marker. Placing a stone now is a symbolic act that shows someone has come to visit. It says "I was here; you are not forgotten."

Visiting Bergen-Belsen this time had less of an impact than visiting Auschwitz-Birkenau, and even Buchenwald, because my sister and I both survived Bergen-Belsen and got out alive and reasonably well. When I was there this time I could see the grass, the heather, and the flowers that everyone else was seeing, but I was also seeing images of the horror I had seen before. That would never change, no matter how many times I went back.

When I see pictures of how the bodies of the dead were thrown and bulldozed into mass graves, I am upset by how little respect was shown to the bodies. It was as if they were discarding a rag or a stone or something they didn't want anymore. I think the British soldiers could have made the SS officers treat the bodies with more respect. I understand the need to have mass graves. What else could they have done?

I came away from Bergen-Belsen with hope in my heart because I saw a lot of young people there, high-school students. The tour guide who was with one group of young people was very kind to take a few minutes to talk to us.

8

SWEDEN

Democracy must be won, and won again. Nazism, Fascism and racism cannot be tolerated. We all share a responsibility as citizens never to remain silent (1998)… Our quest must be to increase our efforts to pass on the legacy of our past to future generations. We must be able to say to our children: There is always a choice. Not to choose is also a choice.

former Swedish Prime Minister
Göran Persson, 2000

Sweden was officially neutral during World War II, so they were not invaded by the Germans, as were neighbouring countries Norway and Denmark. They have been criticized for allowing Germany to use Swedish trains to move troops and freight across northern Sweden, and for selling iron ore to Germany, a material that was essential for German's armament industry. They were worried about possible German aggression and believed, in the early years of the war, that cooperation with Germany was necessary to preserve this precarious neutrality. For several years Sweden put its considerable economic resources at the disposal of the Reich, but after 1943, having been warned by the Allies about the dangers of continuing to do business with Germany, gradually reduced its political and commercial ties with Germany and established closer ties with the Allies. This helped reduce the stigma of collaboration. After the war, the Riksbank, the Swedish central bank, examined gold it had received from the Nazis in payment for exports and returned about 13 tons, concluding that it had been stolen from Belgium and the Netherlands.

Walking a very fine line between cooperating with the Germans and provoking them into invading their country, Sweden managed to save large numbers of Jews, including their own, from being taken to Nazi concentration camps. In the summer of 1943, the German authorities in Denmark decided to send all the Danish Jews to the camps.

The Danes managed to transport 8,000 Jews across the water to Sweden, where they were granted asylum and taken in by Swedes. In addition, up to 50,000 Norwegians were smuggled into Sweden and given asylum there.

The Swedish ambassador in Budapest, Raoul Wallenberg, along with diplomats from several other neutral countries, saved thousands of Jews in Hungary by issuing protective passes to them. He knew from past experience that both the German and Hungarian authorities liked flashy symbols, so he had the passes printed in yellow and blue, with the coat of arms of the Three Crowns of Sweden in the middle, and added the appropriate stamps and signatures. Although these passes had no real value whatsoever in international law, Wallenberg went to great lengths to ensure that the Germans accept them as valid documents, and they did. Shortly after the Russians arrived in Hungary, they arrested Wallenberg, for reasons that still remain unclear. He was never seen again and is assumed to have died in a Soviet prison.

Sweden's neutrality enabled Count Folke Bernadotte, a relative of the royal family and vice-president of the Swedish Red Cross, to relay back to Sweden important information about what was happening in Germany. During the autumns of 1943 and 1944, he organized prisoner exchanges that brought home 11,000 prisoners from Germany via Sweden. Just before the end of the war, he led a rescue operation and transported interned Norwegians, Danes, and western European inmates from German concentration camps to hospitals in Sweden. Around 15,000 people, including several thousand Jews, were taken to safety in the "White Buses" (painted white with a red cross on the side).

Many Swedish nobles used personal connections and wealth to take in, and find temporary Swedish homes for children from neighbouring countries (mainly Denmark and Finland).

In 1945, the Swedish Red Cross brought 6,000 prisoners rescued from Bergen-Belsen to Sweden. One of these people was Eva Olsson.

> Hear this, ye old men, and give ear, all ye inhabitants of the land. Hath this been in your days, or even in the days of your fathers? Tell ye your children of it, and let your children tell their children, and their children another generation.
>
> (Joel 1:3)

Early in 1997, an alarming report was published in Sweden, showing that more than 10 percent of Swedish students did not know about the Holocaust. In addition, a large percentage of teenagers expressed skepticism as to whether the Holocaust had actually occurred or questioned the scale on which it had occurred. In 1998, Prime Minister Göran Persson and the Swedish government organized "Living History," an information campaign of knowledge about and remembrance of the Holocaust. They commissioned a book, Tell Ye Your Children: A Book about the Holocaust in Europe, 1933-1945*, *written by Stéphane Bruchfeld and Paul Levine, that was to be distributed free to all households and schools requesting a copy. They had expected that between 20,000 and 40,000 copies would be ordered, but by 2008 over 1.5 million Swedish households have ordered it, nearly 60% of the population.*

Now available in eight languages and distributed in 14 countries, 2,500,000 copies are currently in print. Tell Ye Your Children *covers the rise of anti-Semitism in Europe and the Nazis' genocide of the Jews, as well as their mass murder of Gypsies, gays, and the developmentally disabled. It mixes text and graphic photographs of the Holocaust, and attempts to explain how the unimaginable became reality. The book describes what human beings are capable of doing to other human beings when democratic values have been destroyed and replaced by an ideology advocating intolerance, hate, and violence.*

* available online at http://www.levandehistoria.se/files/engelska.pdf

I was overwhelmed by the ferry we took this time from Travemunde in Germany to Trelleborg in Sweden. It was a luxury ferry compared to the one that took us to Sweden 62 years ago. Perhaps the other one was normally a cargo ferry or something like that, because it had no chairs or beds. We had to lie on the floor, and the sea was rough, so we kept rolling into each other all night. The food we got on board was very bland, kind of like Jell-O, but that was okay, because our stomachs weren't able to handle much food anyway after months of being starved. Quite a few refugees died after arriving in Sweden because their stomachs couldn't process food anymore.

What was I feeling on the ferry this time? Was I happy to leave Germany? Yes. Everybody was very kind and very nice, but for some reason I felt I didn't belong there and wanted to get out as soon as I could. Also, after travelling 17 days in Hungary, Romania, Poland, and Germany, revisiting the camps where my family died and where I was imprisoned, I was anxious to get to Sweden. I wanted to see what it was like now, and express my gratitude for the caring, compassionate way they had treated the refugees after the war.

As we approached Sweden I was wondering what I was going to find after being away 56 years. I knew that Tyra, my mother-in-law, was alive, and I had two sisters-in-law, Gunnel and Marianne, who were very young when my husband Rude and I left in 1951 to come to Canada. I wasn't sure what their reaction would be to seeing me again. I wondered what Gustavsberg was going to be like, where I had first worked, where I met Rude, and where we lived after we got married. I have a lot of happy memories of the two of us there. But I couldn't help thinking about how tragically things turned out, with Rude dying in 1964 after a car accident. Although Rude couldn't be with me this time, I know his spirit and his love were there.

I knew there were going to be challenges going back to Sweden, but not as many as when I first went there in 1945. At that time, we were excited to be getting out of hell and going to heaven. But there was also fear—fear of a new country, a foreign language. We didn't know how we were going to make a living. I was especially petrified because I had never been to school, so I didn't even know how to write or read. How was I going to survive with so little knowledge of anything? But while that part wasn't a very comfortable experience, it was just amazing to live in a country where people accepted us and cared for us. They provided us with clothing, work, and housing. We were not expected to pay rent until we had worked long enough to earn some money and get on our feet.

In October 1945, about four months after we arrived, I met Rude, my husband-to-be. Of course I didn't know that then. But to have him as a friend at that time meant that I didn't feel so isolated. He helped me learn the Swedish language, and that helped me a great deal to adjust to life in this new country, because I was able to live on my own and carry on a normal daily life.

One of the challenges this time was meeting Rude's family, whom I hadn't seen for 56 years. There were a lot of emotions on both sides. I'm sure it was difficult for them, remembering the son and brother who left them all those years ago. Before we had left Canada, I had sent copies of my autobiography to them so they could catch up with what my life had been like. For a long time I hadn't been able to understand why they hadn't contacted me or my son, and I thought, "Well, maybe they didn't want to be bothered." I told Marianne and Gunnel that I sometimes wondered if the fact that I was Jewish had made a difference. The warmth of my reception this time convinced me that I was wrong about that. They told me that they had tried to locate us in Canada years ago, but had not been successful. Marianne went to a lot of trouble to come to see me, and Gunnel's hospitality was wonderful the whole time I was there. I really appreciated what both of them did very much.

When I arrived in Stockholm this time, I felt lost, like a total stranger, not knowing what to expect. But the next morning, after a nice breakfast and a chat with a lovely lady who spoke English, I felt better. Later, Ron and I took a boat tour of Stockholm, one of the last of the season. That was nice because I could see some of the places Rude and I used to go to when we came to Stockholm. After that I didn't feel so lost anymore.

While we were on the boat, we saw the Raoul Wallenberg memorial near the synagogue, so we decided to walk to it when the boat tour ended. Wallenberg is a national hero in Sweden and in the Jewish community worldwide, because when he was the Swedish ambassador in Budapest, he and a few other diplomats from neutral countries issued protective passes to thousands of Jews. These papers made it look like the people who got them were under Swedish protection, and since Sweden was neutral in the war, the Nazis and the Hungarian Arrow Cross couldn't touch them. He and the other diplomats from neutral countries are credited with saving thousands of people by their actions.

At the memorial, we met some young people from Norway who were studying in Stockholm, and a few people from the local Jewish community, and they told us about a reception that evening, where the Jewish community was going to honour former prime minister Göran Persson (1996-2006) for his work on behalf of the Jews. We went back to the Jewish community centre that night to see the presentation and hear him speak. As one of the Jewish refugees the Swedes took in, I was very, very impressed with the speech he gave. He did an amazing job. After his speech I went up, introduced myself to him, and thanked him for what Sweden had done for us.

I'm also very impressed that the Swedish government commissioned the book, *Tell Ye Your Children,* and made it available free to every household and school in Sweden. I wonder why that sort of thing doesn't happen in Ontario or the rest of Canada? The Swedes were very compassionate and caring towards the refugees they took in after the war, and they're teaching their young people so they won't ever forget what happened in the Holocaust. This gives me hope for the future, a very positive feeling. I was very happy and proud to be part of that community that night. I really felt I belonged there.

My sister-in-law Marianne took a 40-minute bus ride from Gustavsberg to our hotel in Stockholm to see me. This was the only time we could get together, because she was leaving the next day for a week's holiday in Turkey, and she wouldn't be coming home until the night we were leaving Sweden. It was nice to see her and not difficult to recognize her as soon as she came into the lobby. I have a picture of her when she was four, taken around the time we left Sweden. I don't know how much she remembers, but she

Marianne

from her mother. It was obvious she wanted to see me, and we had a really great reunion that I will always remember. I talked to Marianne after we had been home for a while and I asked her if she had read my autobiography. She said she had read the part about Rude. She tried to read other parts too, but some of the things were difficult for her to understand in English.

Rude's two young sisters were not very happy when we left Sweden in 1951. In fact, nine-year-old Gunnel said, "You're taking my big brother away." That made me feel guilty, because my husband didn't have any reason to leave Sweden; he did it for me. Now one might ask, "If things were so good in Sweden, why did you leave?" The Korean War was going on

Gunnel

then and the Russians were right beside us in Finland. That frightened me and many of the other refugees, because we didn't want to go through another war. The Swedes weren't concerned about that because they hadn't been in a war for many years, but for those of us who had just got out of a war, that fear was very real.

I was worried about what would happen if there was another war, afraid that I wouldn't be able to deal with it. Although I did have a caring husband who was very supportive, I still feared having to go through the horrors I had endured so recently and being left alone again. I knew that this fear was a carry-over in my mind from the earlier atrocities, but I still had to work hard to try and put it behind me. I realized later that the lives of survivors can never be normal again, because our minds will always return to the gas chamber, the fire pits, the death marches, the piles of dead bodies, typhoid, lice, starvation, and dehumanization. I didn't have any physical problems—my scars were emotional.

Seeing how worried I was about the possibility of another

war, Rude suggested that we go to Canada for six months as tourists and see how we liked it. He liked it, so we stayed. For a long time I felt very bad about taking Rude away from Sweden, but I got over it as we settled into our life in Canada.

Seeing Rude's family on this trip and explaining how much I wanted to come back to Sweden helped me a lot.

Ron and I took the train to Tierp, in Uppsala County, north of Stockholm, to visit Gunnel and her husband, Sten Wallinder. They met us at the station, and she was very emotional, hugging me, holding my hands, and touching my face. I was the same, so glad to see

her after all those years. Some people think that Swedes are cool, that they don't touch much, but that wasn't true for Gunnel that day.

We spent several days at their beautiful farm. Their house is a typical Swedish house in many ways. Like the majority of the houses in Sweden, it is painted red and has white trim around the doors and windows. Gunnel explained that the red pigment, called *Falu*

Rödfärg [falu red] in Swedish, is a bi-product of the copper mining industry in Sweden, making it inexpensive and easily available. The main entrance had a double set of beautiful wooden doors.

In their kitchen they had a huge stove, the kind I had seen in Hungary when I was a child. And of course there was a tablecloth on the table. You know, they don't use placemats, and neither did we at home. No matter how poor you were, you never served a meal without a tablecloth on the table.

Another thing I really liked was the Swedish tradition of having lamps in the windows. Sometimes there would be no other lights in the room. It's very attractive, very welcoming. I would love to have that at my place in Bracebridge, but I have no windowsills. In the old days the Swedes often had a petroleum lamp in the window. The hotel we stayed at in Gustavsberg had a small lighthouse lamp in the window.

I met their son Lars, his wife Elisabeth, and their sons Tobias and Jonas for the first time. Lars runs the farm and a logging operation there, and Elisabeth is a teacher. They seemed really excited to meet me, and I felt very welcome there.

Sten is sweet guy, very compassionate, understanding, relaxed, not highly charged or driven. It was easy to speak to him, even though there were a few things I didn't understand because he has a different Swedish dialect. And at 69 years old, he's very fit. He has skied 12 Vassaloppets—90 km ski races—since he turned 50.

Shortly after we arrived at Gunnel and Sten's, she called my son Jan in Canada. It had been 35 years since Gunnel last talked to him. He visited Sweden for two months that summer, and lived with his grandmother. Marianne and Gunnel were very, very good to him then. They took him to Norway and Finland

and drove him around everywhere. The contact was good for him. Now they're all very happy we have reconnected. It will be so much easier for any of us to visit the other from now on. I'm hoping they will visit us in Bracebridge soon.

Gunnel gave me one of her dalahorses, to give to Alexandra, and I bought two others to give to Brenna and Rudy. I had

one that was Rude's, but I gave that one to Jan, many years ago. The *dalahäst* has been around for hundreds of years and is often considered to be a symbol for Sweden itself.

I had been very pleased to hear that my mother-in-law, Tyra, was still alive—97 years old! Gunnel was concerned that the three-hour drive north from Tierp to Rättvik might be too long a trip for me, but I assured her it would be fine, because I really wanted to see Tyra. It was a beautiful day as Sten drove us north through countryside that looked like Ontario. It reminded me that Rude used to say how much Canada looked like Sweden.

Tyra looked very healthy, and walked well, although she was

a little bit hard of hearing. I was also impressed by what a good appetite she had. When Sten and Ron went for a walk and Gunnel went to shop for lunch, Tyra and I were alone. We went down memory lane, looking at pictures I had brought of my son, his wife, and my grandchildren, and talking about the past. Some of it was very difficult for her. She kept repeating, "If only things had been different then ... if only." She meant that if she had had money she could have helped us when we were in dire straits in our early years in Canada. She felt bad that she couldn't help ... that she couldn't do things in the past that she would like to have done for her son. She thanked me and said how much she appreciated what I had done for Rude. I told her it wasn't work for me; it was done with love.

She was really amazed at all the things I was doing, like the presentations I make at schools, and she asked, "How does it come that you are so talented?" When she saw my name on my autobiography, *Unlocking the Doors*, she asked how I had become Dr. Olsson. Gunnel explained to her that it was an honorary degree I had been awarded in 2005 by Nipissing University for my work with schools.

Although it was a very emotional reunion for both of us, I was very pleased that I'd made the commitment to go and see her. The morning after our visit, I woke up with a very peaceful feeling, knowing I'd done the right thing. It is good that I did visit her then, because five days after we arrived back in Canada, I heard from her daughter that Tyra had died

of pneumonia on October 20, 2007. It was such a shock, because she had seemed so healthy when we were there.

In November Tyra was buried beside her two sisters in a family plot in a very peaceful graveyard near Furudal, overlooking the lake. Gunnel and Sten had taken us there after our visit with Tyra in Rättvik.

Seeing the Stockholm City Hall was an emotional moment for me, because it took me back to that wonderful Saturday—July 9,

1949—when Rude and I got married. I was in my glory that day. They say that all brides are beautiful, but I really felt very beautiful that day, especially with such a beautiful man standing beside me. Rude and I took the bus into Stockholm and had lunch with his Aunt Hilda and her husband. Then Aunt Hilda took me to a salon for brides, where one of the ladies did my hair and fitted me for a white dress and a short veil. Later, Rude arrived at the salon with a bouquet of red and white carnations. Rude's parents, Tyra and Leonard, joined us at the Stockholm City Hall at three o'clock in the afternoon for the brief ceremony.

After that we went to a hotel where a reception dinner and dance for 50 people had been arranged. The refugee girls I worked with were all invited, and some of Rude's relatives also attended. The dinner was delicious and my father-in-law supplied the table with imported French cognac. The hotel gardens were ideal for taking wedding pictures. But things have changed a lot since then. It's much busier in that location now, with heavy traffic on the roads around the hall, and the gardens are gone. We spent our honeymoon at Rude's grandparents' home in Furudal, a small village in northern Sweden.

Being back at the Stockholm City Hall again brought back a lot of memories, joy and sadness mixed together as I walked in front of that gorgeous building. I felt privileged to have had the opportunity to be there again. I just wish ... but wishing never makes it so. I'm sure Rude knows that I was there; I felt his spirit with me. I certainly have no regrets, because the years I was married to Rude were the best years of my life. I couldn't have wanted for a better husband, a more loving and caring human being. Sadly, on February 26, 1962, while driving to work along Major Mackenzie Drive, my husband was hit head-on by a man driving a truck under the influence of alcohol. After struggling to regain his health for several years, Rude died on September 24, 1964, shortly before he would have turned 38. I am so blessed that I have been able to keep my husband's spirit alive in my autobiography and talking about him in my presentations.

Being able to revisit places Rude and I had gone together when we came into Stockholm brought back fond memories. As Ron and I were walking on Kungsgatan (King) Street, I recognized the market where Rude and I used to shop on Saturdays. I remember the old Swedish farmers who used to have stalls there. The biggest change I found there now was that there were no native Swedes selling produce at the market. One chap I talked to was Bulgarian, and the other vendors were multinational, from all over Europe.

When I saw the finger mushrooms, it reminded me of when Rude and I used to wander into the woods to look for mushrooms. He knew the ones that were not poisonous. He always made sure that I had high boots on when we went into the woods because there were snakes, and I was petrified of snakes. One Saturday I was buying shrimps at the market, and the guy who was serving us was so fascinated with the beautiful leather shopping bag I was carrying that he filled it up with shrimps. When Rude went to pay he couldn't understand why it was so expensive. He thought he was just paying for one kilo of shrimps. I brought that bag to Canada and I still have it today.

Rude and I used to shop for ladies' clothes and shoes at the department store beside the market. He had very good taste and was particular about the kind of clothes I wore, so he always came with me when I shopped. I particularly remember a beautiful green dress and a cocoa-brown two-piece suit that we bought at this store. I brought all those dresses with me to Canada and wore them until I started to put on weight. Then I gave them away and let somebody else wear them. I also recognized the street where my husband had bought me a beautiful ring and a necklace. Those are good memories, and Rude was with me in spirit as I revisited those places.

After we had spent two nights at Gunnel and Sten's farm, Gunnel drove us to Gustavsberg. It was great to have the opportunity to revisit the place where my husband and I lived, and also where I worked in the porcelain factory. We were able to take a look at the factory, but it was a big disappointment, as it isn't the way it used to be when I worked there. It's smaller, and they don't make a lot of the things we used to make because it's cheaper to import them from China. The porcelain that we used to make in Gustavsberg is now very expensive to buy when you can find it.

Visiting Gustavsberg was a bittersweet experience, and I could hardly recognize the place anymore. When we are away from a place we think that somehow it has remained

the same. But as I found out when I visited Satu Mare, time has a way of moving on and things change. For example, the first place I lived in with a group of refugee girls had been torn down just a month before our visit. There were 2,000 people in Gustavsberg when I lived there before, and now the population is 8,000. A lot of the people work in Stockholm and commute, so there are many new apartment buildings and roads. I shouldn't be surprised that nothing is the same as it used to be, in Sweden or anywhere else. Oh well, at least I still had my memories of how it used to be.

We drove and walked around Gustavsberg, visiting the places

I had lived in, alone and with Rude. The most emotional part for me was looking at the balcony of the apartment we had lived in before moving to Canada. Interestingly, Marianne lives in the apartment next door to the one we had. We went to the church where our marriage banns had been announced, and I lit a candle in memory of Rude.

It was a big surprise when Marianne told me that Edith, a very good friend all those years ago, still lived in Gustavsberg. She had also been a prisoner in Bergen-Belsen, but we didn't know each other there. We had lived in the same building in Gustavsberg, and Rude and I used to chum around with her and Alf, her Swedish boyfriend. Sometimes the four of us would go to the Jewish social organization in Stockholm for

parties and dances, and there was never any question of Rude or Alf being accepted in the group.

Gunnel, Ron, and I went to Edith's house in the afternoon and she served us coffee and cakes. She's married to a very nice man, Jaroslav Tupy, who arrived in Sweden from Czechoslovakia in 1948. I'm pleased that she seems to be having a very good life. She's very artistic; she does a lot of beautiful work using natural materials. Her home was filled with books and artwork. It was really great to see her and to catch up after all these years.

That evening we had dinner at Mat's apartment, Gunnel's other son, who works for a bank. Marianne's two daughters, Suzanne, who's a teacher, and Ulrika, who works at the local police station, also joined us. After we had dinner we sat at the table and they looked at pictures I had brought from Canada. It was a very lovely evening, a positive side of the visit.

Suzanne explained that they were very excited and happy to see me. She said she had been sorry we'd lost contact and they're happy we reconnected. Mats and the girls really wanted to hear more about my life and asked lots of questions. In the six years I lived in Sweden, I never talked about myself. One time when we were up in Furudal, two of Rude's aunts and some other people came to dinner. When they

started asking me questions about my past life, Rude made a gesture with his hand across his throat [enough!], and ended that right away. He was very protective of me.

Another time, a friend of his named Charlie opened his cigarette box and gave me a cigarette. I didn't smoke, but I took it because I didn't want to be impolite. Before Charlie had a chance to light it, Rude took the cigarette out of my hand and gave it back, because he didn't want me to get hooked. He didn't like me to wear lipstick or powder, so I rarely did. He said he preferred the natural look, and I trusted his judgment because he had such good taste.

Visiting Furudal was very powerful emotionally for me, very sad because it brought back an awful lot of memories of Rude. I could have broken down several times there, but I didn't want to do that. Rude and I first went to his grandparents' house [Tyra's parents] in Furudal in 1946, a year after we met. We also went there for two weeks on our

honeymoon, and his family had a big reception for us. It was a very important time for both of us. It was such a beautiful place to be, kind of a dream place, because there was no stress, no fighting or bickering. Rude had been raised there by his grandparents, Agatha and Jan Eric, so he especially enjoyed being there with someone he loved. My son is named after his great-grandfather, and Gunnel and Marianne still call him that.

The house sits on a hill, overlooking a private lake. We often used to go down to the lake and sail around all day. One Saturday the family decided that I should make a pot of chicken soup for everyone, because they had never

Rude's Grandparents

had soup made in the Hungarian style. We slaughtered and plucked a chicken, and I left the pot of chicken soup simmering on the stove. Rude decided to take me out on a small sailboat, saying we would just be gone out for an hour or so. However, there was no wind to come back, and we were gone the whole afternoon. When we got home, there was no soup left in the pot; it had all simmered away. His uncle said to him, "You were crazy to do that. How could you take her out on that boat?"

Rude just wanted to show me his life, how he liked to live, and what he liked to do. He loved fishing, so he taught me how to fish and we used to go fishing a lot. Like most Scandinavian people, he loved the woods and the water. In my album is a picture of that house in 1949, showing the family sitting on the steps.

The woman who lives there now let us go into the house and walk around. Understandably, she has newer, modern furniture. Rude's grandparents had the real old kind of furniture, including a very old wood stove that they cooked on. I can still see the coffee pot that never came off the stove. They drank coffee all day. Rude's grandmother would pour a little coffee into a saucer with a sugar cube and sip it. I had never seen anyone drink coffee like that before. It was also the first time I saw anyone peel a lemon and eat the lemon wedges. Lemon, instead of an orange.

They had pigs there too, so they had a lot of pork. They churned their own butter, using milk from their own cow, and that was very hard work, as I discovered when it was my turn to do the churning.

It was a very nice life in Furudal, especially since I had just got out of hell. There was peace and quiet all around us there— no guards, no police, no barbed wire. It was a great feeling being surrounded by people who loved and accepted me. Being back there this time brought back many memories of the good times we'd had.

Saying goodbye to Gunnel when she brought us back to our hotel in Stockholm was very difficult for both of us. For her, I was a connection to her brother, whom she didn't know very well because she was so young when we left for Canada. For me, reconnecting with her, meeting her family, and spending time at her home created wonderful new memories for me to take back to Canada with me. Gunnel and Sten came back

to Stockholm the day before we left for Canada, and we spent a great day walking, visiting the Jewish Centre, and having a long dinner together. Thankfully, our goodbye that day wasn't as emotionally difficult as the one a few days earlier.

My time in Sweden was bittersweet, with memories of my arrival there as a refugee and my life with Rude mixed in with reconnecting with his family, both old and young. For me, Sweden had been heaven after the hell of the concentration camps, and being back there was the perfect—and most appropriate—way to complete this journey.

9

AFTER THE JOURNEY

If all this suffering does not help us to broaden
our horizon, to attain a greater humanity by
shedding all trifling and irrelevant issues, then
it will all have been for nothing.

Etty Hillesun

Was the trip worth it? Absolutely. It was a journey I thought I would never take, but I am pleased that I chose to take it. I have more sadness now than I did before, and I know that after what I experienced on this journey, my life will never be the same. My mind is working overtime now, always searching for more information, more answers. It's an endless search; sometimes the more you search, the more you want to know. I am dealing with it as I deal with everything else, on a day-to-day basis.

The journey has made me even more committed to making presentations about my life, especially to schools. I came away from the trip with the feeling that I am not doing enough, that I should be doing more. Seeing what I did on this trip has reinforced in me the importance of showing people what hate can do. I hope my story will convince students of the importance of compassion, love, and respect for all mankind.

One of the reasons the trip was so positive was that I got to go back and think about and say the things I never had a chance to say sixty years ago. I'm glad that I was finally able to go back to my hometown and the concentration camps sixty years later, even though there was no trace of my family in any of those places.

I paid a huge price in retracing my life. Although I didn't realize it before, part of the reason I never wanted to go back was that I didn't want to face my fears of what I'd find and what I might have to deal with after the trip. I have had a lot of dreams since we got back, and that doesn't seem to be getting any better for some reason. I hoped that in time I'd process all the feelings I had brought back with me and find some peace, but I haven't been able to do that yet. While we were on the trip there wasn't much time to process what I was seeing and feeling. I don't know yet what the long-term impact of the trip will be, but perhaps when this book is finished and I can read it and watch Don Gray's documentary DVD *Stronger Than Fire: The Eva Olsson Story*, I will be able to put it in the right perspective.

It took courage for me to step back into that darkness, to see things I had not seen while I was a prisoner, but I came away with a new perspective. Seeing these new things has added new memories to the old memories and reminded me of the magnitude of what happened back then. This time I was actually able to see everything—I didn't just read about it or imagine what it must have been like. This time I got to walk in those places and see those things with my own eyes. When I went into the gas chamber, I did not see an empty room. I saw people I knew standing in there, being murdered in there.

When the Holocaust was happening, I was part of it, so I could not see the full extent of what they were trying to do. On this journey, I was able to revisit where and how the Nazis murdered 11 million people, and that has given me a different perspective on the whole thing. Six million Jews … five million other people … These are just numbers, like telephone numbers in a phone book, until you stop and think about them being murdered one by one.

My feelings, my life, and my message have all changed because of the trip. When I first got back, I couldn't deal with it. I couldn't even go outside and face people for the first few days. If someone asked me about the trip, I started to cry. All I could say was "devastating," and walk away. But the best thing I did was get back to work, even though at first I broke down when I opened my mouth.

The Holocaust changes your life and your whole perspective. It forces us to look at the dark side of humanity, because these were human beings who did these things, not animals. Animals don't do those things. Animals kill when they are hungry or threatened, not because of hate. These were human beings who used their free will to choose to torture and murder millions of people.

One is forced to the conviction that those who did these horrible things saw nothing wrong in them; perhaps they were actually proud of their efficiency in producing death. These [Nazis] are not as other humans; they are satanic. Though they have a veneer of Christianity, deep down they must still be barbarians—in saying this one is unfair to the barbarian because there is a scientific refinement about these horrors which barbarians, uncouth and wild, living in a primitive state, could not invent. (From a letter written in April 1945, by Georges Vanier, the Canadian Ambassador to France)

How clever the Nazis thought they were to organize this killing machine. I don't know if most people can comprehend just how carefully the Nazis maneuvered everything, how they lured people—"Pack a suitcase; you're going to work in a brick factory … Hurry up, have a shower. When you come out, you're going to have coffee." They didn't want people to panic and cause trouble before they killed them. A few weeks ago, when I was watching a seven-hour documentary on the Holocaust, I saw more details about how the Nazis went from country to country and arranged to transport and exterminate their Jews. Some countries even paid the Nazis to take their Jews away. Humanity sunk so low then, buried in hate and anger. It's hard to imagine how they could sink any lower.

Perhaps we all have a dark side to some degree. But never have I heard of people who hated and chose to live on the dark side of humanity as much as the Nazis. Never before in history had there been such a premeditated attempt to annihilate an entire group of people.

One night, about four months after I arrived home from the trip, I broke down big time. It could have been because I was making a goulash soup, and it reminded me of my mom, how she used to brown the onion and garlic and other ingredients. People die of old age, people die of disease, people die of unfortunate accidents … young people, old people, people of all ages. I know many people died in the war, but this was my mom. The way she died is still the most difficult thing for me to come to terms with. That night I felt I couldn't hold it in any longer; I had to let it out. Sometimes I have to cry when I'm alone, just to relieve some of that tension that's always there. I feel like I've been alone for a very long time.

I lost it again when I was making a presentation to an audience in Winnipeg last February. I started to cry when I was talking about my mother waiting to go to the gas chambers, thinking what her last moments were like as she was watching her grandchildren suffocate before she did. However, I don't feel bad for crying, because I'm not ashamed of my tears. People need to see that I can laugh and I can cry.

While I was walking around Auschwitz-Birkenau, I just wanted to scream. I felt like I was screaming inside! I had that same feeling when I got to Satu Mare, my hometown. I wanted to look up at the sky and call out to my mom. But there were crowds of people around me then and I had to control my feelings so people wouldn't think I was crazy. Sometimes when I'm at home on the Muskoka River in Bracebridge, I have thought that I'd like to take a boat out into the middle of the river and shout as loudly as I can, so that my voice would travel all over the world.

At some point you have to decide whether you are going to let your pain control you or you are going to control your pain. I have to live with the pain, but I want to control my own destiny. I look around and see people in pain trying to fix it with alcohol and medication. They are not dealing with the pain; they're too afraid to deal with it. I had to overcome the fears that had kept me silent for 50 years, and face them head on.

So how should we deal with tragedies? We have to make choices as to how we're going to deal with the good and bad that happens to us. I have made the choice to deal with the tragedies in my life, like what happened to my family in the Holocaust, and Rude's death. We have to accept responsibility for our actions and not blame God or somebody else. The choices we made yesterday affect us today, and the choices we are making right now will affect us tomorrow. After my husband died, I made a choice, a commitment to be there for my son, the one blessing I still had left. I cannot bring back the ones who died but I can be there for him whenever he needs me. That's how I dealt with my tragedies.

People often ask me if any members of my family were with me on the trip, and I can honestly say I'm glad none of them were. It would have been very difficult for my son or any of my grandchildren to see what I went through on that journey. I don't know whether any of them wish they had gone with me this time. It's possible they may want to go sometime in the future, perhaps when I'm not around anymore. My grandson Rudy says he will be going there, possibly when he's in Europe with his friends.

When I raised our son, I didn't want to tell him much about my past. Yes, he knew I was a Holocaust survivor, but I didn't share any of the details with him until he was at university and asked me about it. I felt, "What's the point? Why should he suffer because of what the Nazis put us through?" I guess I was trying to protect him. I found out two years ago that he was also trying to protect me then, not telling me that he had been called "you Jew" when he was in high school in Richmond Hill. I have learned that none of us can completely protect ourselves or those we love from every danger.

When I was in Ottawa a vice-principal introduced me to a little boy who was very upset because he's German and some other kids were bullying him. He felt better after I hugged him and said, "There will always be bullies. You have to learn to walk away from them." When I think about that little boy, I wonder what message the Nazis—many of them were parents and grandparents—passed down to the next generation? That it's okay to murder millions of people because you don't like them? That some people are worth less than others? Young Germans we spoke to on the trip told us it's hard for them, because they have to live with that history they've inherited. For some, it's easier to live in denial, insisting the Holocaust didn't even happen.

It has gone through my mind a few times that this journey is not yet over. Perhaps I have some unfinished footsteps to take there and should go back to Auschwitz-Birkenau and Satu Mare because they still have the most power over me. Auschwitz-Birkenau is like a living museum. The air, the smell, the tears are still there—I don't think it's possible for the atmosphere there to change. While I was on the trip, I was under such constant emotional stress that it took over the whole experience of being there. There was so much packed into those 28 days that it wasn't possible to give each part my full attention. Perhaps if I went back, I would look for different things, and I would see things differently. As I said before, my mind is still looking for more information, but I realize that going back probably wouldn't change that. I will probably never get the answers I seek, so I don't think that I will ever take this journey again.

I knew that our homes in Satu Mare wouldn't still be there, but I was really hoping that I could at least find the courtyard where we used to live, so I could go inside and stand there. But that was gone too, and a two-storey building is being built there now. I wonder if I should have gone and knocked on the door of the house on the corner. Or the big house that the landlord owned and his father lived in next door to us. Perhaps I could have gone to number 17, the white house where I used to sneak in to listen to the daughter playing a beautiful black piano. The woman who lived there was a year younger than me. I wonder if any of them survived the Holocaust? I guess I will never know.

I have read that some people survived the concentration camps partly because they were able to focus outside themselves and their own survival. This was true for me. During the Holocaust, I always had to think of my sister; it was very important to have her with me, because she was all I had left of my family. In the factory, I used to hide her in the foreman's corner behind sheet metal. If somebody came she grabbed a broom and began sweeping the floor. Even at the end, in the darkest days in Bergen-Belsen, I thought, "I cannot die here, because if I die, who will look after her?" I felt responsible because I'm nearly three years older than her. I also reached out and tried to comfort a couple of other girls who were in trouble emotionally. Yes, that's definitely part of survival, there's no question about it. It's harder to survive if you're just thinking about yourself.

I have had the ability to focus outside myself as long as I can remember. I always enjoyed helping others when I was young, but part of the reason I did it was selfish—I wanted to get out of the restrictive religious environment in our house. After Rude died, I drove people to the hospital or the doctor's office for appointments. In Richmond Hill a Swedish woman asked me to go to a convalescent hospital and visit her husband, a Polish man who had lost his legs. He seemed to enjoy the visits, and she was curious to know what we talked about. We used to talk about cars, a subject he was really interested in. My father used to visit people in the hospital, and he said that by doing that you take some of their sickness away when you leave. I like that thought and believe it's true. Also, visiting these people helped me appreciate what I had.

An English woman told me that in England they stopped teaching the Holocaust because it might upset the Muslims. I was shocked. How would it affect them unless they were there and did something wrong? Otherwise I can't understand why they would be upset.

Some people think that Jews are being favoured if the Holocaust is studied in history classes. That's the argument we hear— "You can't just study Jewish history"—as if the Holocaust was "just Jewish history." Of course there are other atrocities that could be studied, but one doesn't cancel out another. The easy answer is, "Well, we won't teach any of them." But the Holocaust is different because of its magnitude and the fact that never before in written history had there ever been such a premeditated systematic annihilation of a group of people. The first targets in eastern Europe were one and a half million children, because the Nazis didn't want any future generations of Jews. People have to be honest with themselves and have a look at what happened there. The Jews were "chosen" for one thing only: to be annihilated.

Martin Luther preached that the only way to get rid of the Jews was to take away their possessions, burn their homes, and drive them out of Germany. Hitler was taught the same negative views of Jews and used this fear and hatred to stir people up. The Lutheran Church has since apologized for Martin Luther's anti-Semitic beliefs, but unfortunately many people still hold them.

Moreso now than ever before, I realize that having the strength to speak about my life and what I've been through has been a healing process for me and has brought great peace and freedom to my soul. I go out to speak now with a new strength, a new sense of purpose. That's what's most important in my life now. I can never bring my family back, but I can keep their spirit alive. Their voices were silenced by the Nazis, but I feel they are with me when I talk about them.

We need to ask ourselves how we can make tomorrow a better place. On the days when I am speaking at a school, I get up in the morning ready and eager. I go into each school hoping that I will touch at least one child. I want children to have respect for one another.

When I was speaking to an audience of educators in Winnipeg, I told them about a principal I had met. He was waiting while I parked my car at his school, and he said, "I just wanted to tell you that there was bullying on a bus recently. One student was bullied because he has an accent, and another was bullied because he lives in a poor area of the city." That day I started my presentation like this: "I want to share with you something about my life. When I got to Sweden, I didn't speak a word of English. I still have an accent after 56 years. One night I went to a dance with a few other girls from work. I was nervous, because I didn't know how to dance. A man asked me to dance many times, and we got to know each other, even though I didn't yet speak Swedish. I gave myself a chance to know him, and he gave himself a chance to get to know me. He became my best friend and my husband. What happens when you lock yourself in because somebody looks different or has a different religion or has a different accent? You lock other people out, and that might be your best friend that you're locking out."

Sometimes I see presentations that are focused on one victim of a tragedy and go into great detail about the loss that was suffered. Often they are all PowerPoint, never changing one bit. Every word they say, every picture they show, is the same every time. I never guarantee what mine is going to be. Sometimes a quarter of it is the same, sometimes it's different. People have commented that my presentation doesn't come across as a prepared speech, that it sounds authentic and sincere, as if it's the first time I've spoken about it. That's how it feels to me.

My presentation is not just about me and my life. I'm 83 right now and I survived the Holocaust, but the important message I want my audiences to hear is what we are going to do to make sure it doesn't happen again—anywhere, to anyone. If we don't eliminate bullying and help our kids stop hating, we're going backwards to where I came from. That's my fear—not for myself, because at my age I don't fear that— but for my grandchildren and all the other young people.

My presentation changes depending on the audience. I size up my audience and try to tell them what I think they need to hear. When I am talking to younger students, below grade seven, I leave some things out. I talk about the gas chamber, but not in the same depth. I leave out material about Joseph Mengele and the medical experiments, because the younger kids don't need to hear about that.

If a presentation doesn't get the audience to apply the lessons learned in one tragedy to prevent other losses like it, the presentation has limited impact. It would be like me standing on a stage in front of 1,500 educators and talking only about what happened to me or my brother Lazar or my mom. I have to deal with the whole tragedy, not just single out one victim, even though it was a member of my own family. I cannot speak just for me; I have to speak for the 11 million who died in the Holocaust. When I lost a baby, my son lost his sister before she was born. Ten years later, when he lost his father, I lost my husband, my soulmate, the best friend I ever had. But if hearing about what I suffered does not cause my audience to think about the larger issues of hatred, intolerance, and bullying that can lead to genocide, then my work will have been for nothing.

My message is that you can never relax. Hatred of all kinds—racism, bigotry, homophobia, anti-Semitism—is always going to be around. As long as there is hate, genocide will be there too. Hate is based on fear—fear of people who are different, fear of what we don't understand, fear of "them." When you carry hate inside you, it inhibits you and doesn't allow you to be tolerant and respectful of other people. I focus on young peoples' frequent use of the word "hate." I encourage them to say, "I don't like …" rather than "I hate." The pictures from the concentration camps in my presentation show them what real hate can lead to.

People often wonder (and so do I) how I learned to make presentations the way I do. I was never taught to do it. Is this something that was always there but wasn't brought out because I wasn't polished by going to school? When he was 12, Jan said to me: "You should have been a lawyer, Mom. Too bad you weren't educated." So I guess it was there even then.

I was asked recently by a high-school student: "Why are there not others speaking out about today's problems? Why is genocide still happening?" The war ended but genocide didn't end. There is still hunger, starvation, disease. Children are dying or being orphaned every day. Who is looking after them? Who cares? How can we change things? We have to make sure that this young generation take responsibility for their actions.

So I do speak about today's problems too, not just about the Holocaust. We can't change what happened in the past, but it's our responsibility to see that our children have a better future. I try to link what happened in the past and what's happening now in other parts of the world. After they heard me speak, students at one school sent a petition to the prime minister to take action to stop the killing in Darfur. Students are responding to my message by applying it to today's problems.

As parents and educators we have a responsibility to these children we send to schools. If we want to be proud of them when they're adults we need to help them develop good qualities when they're young. Hate isn't one of the qualities we want to see in them. Children absorb and imitate what they see and hear around them, so we have to be better role models. It's not enough just to tell them how to act; we have to show them by our actions.

I started speaking at an age when most people were retiring because I definitely believe I'm needed more now than earlier. Just after the war people were more compassionate and caring. People remembered more, because some of them lost grandfathers, uncles, brothers, or mothers. But as the new generations have come along, that knowledge seems to be vanishing.

A few years ago, a mother spoke to me: "My daughter is reading *The Diary of Anne Frank*, and she's asking me questions. What should I tell her?" I said to her, "Tell her the truth; talk to her about it." She said, "I don't know anything." At home they were never taught about the war. She was educated, but she hadn't learned about it in school either, because there was a period of time when World War II wasn't studied in schools. It's just in the last ten years or so that grade ten students have to study it.

I wasn't ready to speak fifty years ago because I was dealing with a lot of fears. If I had started doing it back then, I'd probably be worn out now and not doing it anymore. I have done 1,700 presentations, to one-and-a-half million people in the past 11 years. There are very few survivors making similar presentations, and not too long from now there won't be any of us left to do it. However, I believe that I am where I'm supposed to be, doing what I was destined to do.

On April 15, the anniversary of the day I was liberated from Bergen-Belsen, my son said to me, "You've done well, Mom, dealing with your sadness and your joy." Well, my joy is here—my grandchildren, my beautiful son, who's a great human being. I really am blessed to be here in Bracebridge, living on the Muskoka River. In spite of all the sadness I have experienced, I have found joy, love, and peace living here. I wouldn't want to live anywhere else. I travel a lot, and when I come back after being away a week or more, I say, "Thank God I am home." This is home. Being able to stand on the banks of the river is good for my soul. My husband taught me how to fish when I lived in Sweden, so when I have time, I like to fish here too.

It was a difficult time for me when my grandchildren came along, because it reminded me of my own mother going to the gas chamber with her grandchildren. They never got to experience all the beauty that the universe has provided for us. But helping raise my grandchildren when they were young has helped provide balance in my life.

When I was working at a restaurant years ago, a woman suggested that I could work more and make more money if my daughter-in-law put my grandchildren in a daycare. I said to her, "If I only eat once a day, I will never give away to anyone else the joy of spending time with my grandchildren." Also, my grandchildren would have missed the opportunity to get to know their grandmother. I could not have lived with myself knowing my grandchildren were in a daycare centre. It's not that there's anything wrong with a daycare centre; it's just that after losing most of my family in the Holocaust, I wanted to spend as much time as possible with them.

The trip renewed my commitment to continue speaking as often as I can, for as long as I can. When children ask me if I'm afraid something like the Holocaust could happen again, I say, "Yes, it can, but if you don't want that, you have to help me by spreading love, not hate. Together we can make a difference."

EPILOGUE

Her courage in breaking her silence and her
dedication to leading a life committed to teaching
peace and justice is a gift to humanity.

Testimonial from San Diego University

The effects of Eva's journey are still reverberating throughout her life today. When she first returned home, she wasn't sure she could continue to speak as often as she had before. The emotions were too raw, the memories of what she had lost too fresh to speak about out loud.

I'm glad I went back, but it was devastating. I felt like someone had taken the air out of me ... like a burst balloon ... hollow, empty. The whole thing was overpowering.

But within a few weeks, Eva's lifelong ability to turn a negative into a positive kicked in, and she felt a new commitment to speak to whoever would listen. Between January and June 2008, Eva made 83 presentations. Making her presentation now takes a greater emotional toll than it did before the trip, but Eva is prepared to pay this price because the feedback she gets from audience members tells her how important it is for them to hear it. She realizes that her message — of forgiveness, tolerance, compassion, of not being a bystander when bad things are happening — is more important than ever.

Every year I drive between 34,000 and 36,000 kilometres to make my presentation. My son suggested that I should focus more on speaking at conferences rather than schools so I wouldn't have to drive so much, but I asked him, "Who's going to speak to the little guy?" The young people need to hear my message even more than older people.

206

Over the years, I've received thousands of letters and testimonials about how my presentation has affected people who heard it. I'm so grateful to people for telling me. If I didn't get the feedback I'm getting, from children, educators, and the general public, I don't think that at 83 I would be going out to speak as often as I do. Their responses motivate me and keep me going.

In June 2007, Eva spoke at the 9th annual Character Development Conference in San Diego, sponsored by the School of Leadership and Education Sciences Character Development Center.

The University of San Diego campus is still resonating with the message of tolerance and hope shared by Eva Olsson in her keynote presentation on June 22, 2007.

The audience of several hundred was informed, touched deeply, and moved to tears as Eva shared the terrifyingly unforgettable experiences she had as a young girl in Auschwitz. The power and candor of her story invigorates provocative thought and challenges each of us to take a stance against intolerance. Eva brings lingering lessons which emanate from all that she endured and all that she has become in spite of the horrors. Her courage in breaking her silence and her dedication to leading a life committed to teaching peace and justice is a gift to humanity. We recommend Eva as a presenter at any event where the human condition is deeply examined. The observations below capture the overwhelmingly positive response to Eva's presentation.

(University of San Diego)

This was one session of the conference during which I made no attempt to document my reflections. Knowing the subject matter and considering the theater environment, I determined that the most useful and relevant learning I could embrace during this event would take place if I were to simply sit and listen. Of course, I did more than that. Eva Olsson took me to places I had never been. I have read and thought about the Holocaust through many avenues over the course of my life, but never have I had the opportunity to be audience to a story so personal or a message so poignant.

Mrs. Olsson never said the word "Nazi" without adding the descriptor "bullies." This hit me hard as a mother of young children who have had occasion to learn to live with bullies. I think that we as parents sometimes minimize the effects that bullies might have on our children; we want to believe that even the bullies are good kids who just need more love and guidance to direct them down a brighter path. The fact that Nazi youth who started out just as innocent as my own children could have been led to a place from which they could rationalize and justify the barbaric and horrific acts they were perpetrating against Jews – in this speaker's lifetime – filled my heart with dread. It empowered me even more to take personal responsibility for Character Education for today's youth. We can not wait for some other influence to come along with a greater charisma to draw our children toward darkness. Kids must be taught and shown what it means to live an honorable life, and to seek and find the rewards that good living can bring.

After the conference on Friday, I met up with some friends and naturally spoke about the powerful message that Eva Olsson offered that afternoon. I shared her story, and hope that by doing so I can also share her passion for making a difference in this world, for letting go of anger and hatred despite having been brutalized and dehumanized, and for finding the strength of character it must take to relive that wretched story day after day in front of audiences around the world, just to keep the story from becoming urban legend.

(Jacquie Kennedy, Director of Child Development Center at the University of San Diego)

While every aspect of the conference was strong, I was moved to tears when Eva Olsson spoke. I will forever hold the image of her standing on the stage, speaking to us and asking, " How many of you have been bullied, are bullies, or are bystanders?" Bystanders. I know so many adult bystanders in my life, and I must say that the majority of students I teach also fall into this category. So I challenged myself at the end of Eva's speech, and I asked myself, "How can I help children and what must I teach, so that each child will feel empowered and ennobled to no longer be the bystander and to say and do what is right, at all times? That is my challenge! It has become easier for me, as an adult, to speak my mind and to stand up for what is right, but this has taken me 35 years to develop, and I want children to know it resides within them at this very moment.

Eva's presentation was moving and visceral. It truly rocked me to my core and I could hear and feel every ounce of what she wanted to convey. I was taken in by her ability to speak her internal dialogue of a moment in time that had happened years ago. It brought me in and made me feel as if I were standing beside her at that historical minute. Yet, within all of this, when Eva said, "When we lock others out, we lock ourselves in," I could no longer stop the tears. I realized at that very moment that Eva's words were a gift to me and I was truly thankful for her inner strength to tell her story and give herself to each of us. I was encouraged by her strength and thankful for her presence. While I have yet to fully process this, I can say that I lock myself in at times. I must ask myself, "If I do this and my students can sense it, why and how would a child in my class feel like learning from me?" … While this will take a bit more time to analyze, I can say that I feel the need to change, and I will guide my educational practice with what Eva described as the four things that we must teach our children: loving, knowing, being, and accepting. How, and in what manner, has yet to fully reveal itself to me, as I need a bit of quiet time to truly delve into this.

(Anne Fennell, Teacher and Parent, Vista, California)

The highlight of the day was our meeting with Eva Olsson. What a woman! What strength of character! Was she born that way? Did she develop her special character traits due to her circumstances? What is it that forms our character? The ones in charge during Mrs. Olsson's incarceration certainly did not display "quality" character traits. … How can someone who has experienced mankind at its worst not display a form of those horrific traits of character as were imposed upon her ...?

(Tere Tangeman, Educator, Julian, California)

In March 2008, Eva received the following letter after she had spoken at Menno Simons Christian School in Calgary:

Our school was deeply touched by your powerful presentation. Prior to your visit, we had questions from some of our older students about why they should listen to a presentation about something that happened so many years ago—it had no impact on their lives. As teachers we found it difficult to find ways to help our students understand that the Holocaust has had a worldwide ripple effect.

You were able to find a way to make that relevant connection by calling the Nazis what they were—bullies. As a Christian school, we have peacemaking as a priority. We appreciated your ability to tell the story in an honest way, which is an act of peacemaking in itself.

We have spent quite a lot of time discussing your presentation and also doing reflective writing. The image of the empty shoes stuck in my head and after talking about it with my class I asked them to write a piece with that title. What my students wrote is amazing, and I'm including a few of their pieces in this package.

Judy Epp, Teacher, on behalf of the Grade 6 class

Eva received this letter from Jennifer Couvrette, a teacher at Orillia District Collegiate and Vocational Institute:

June 26, 2008

I have had to wait a couple of days before writing to you, just to let the experience of your visit to OD permeate. As Elie Wiesel says, there are not words to describe the experience of living inside death, but as one of the English teachers said, "She found the words, and thank goodness she did. What a powerful presentation."

I wanted to share with you the experience of a couple of our teachers who had not had the opportunity to hear you speak before. One of our male phys ed teachers said that at one point he had to stop watching the students' reactions because it was upsetting him as well. He also believes that it was the most important assembly that we've ever had.

One of the music teachers had a unique experience. She said that she returned to class after the assembly, and for the five minutes that remained before lunch, she and her class just sat in absolute silence. No one felt capable of speech or reflecting on what had just happened. I thought this was a very interesting response, similar to what audiences experienced when they first saw the play, The Diary of Anne Frank, *on stage.*

I was also impacted strongly by your presentation. In some ways, I feel our jobs are quite similar. We both attempt to sensitize students to human history and emotions. The difference between us is that you are successful! It is not just the nature of the teenage years that makes this a difficult task. The school setting also seems to remove the feeling of individuality. These students can often hide in the crowd and remove themselves mentally from what we are trying to teach them. On Wednesday, however, you reached every person in that gym, but without destroying their youthful hope and optimism. If they were tempted to lose faith in humanity because of the harsh realities of history, they replaced that despair with hope in you. What you have endured, and what you are doing allows them to look back on horror and still turn forward again.

This is a heavy task you have given them, and it gives me hope to see them take it to heart. Thanks so much for your presence at ODCVI.

In December 2007, Eva received a phone call from the office of the Lieutenant Governor of Ontario, informing her that she was to be inducted into The Order of Ontario, the province's highest official honour. The award recognizes Ontarians who have made an outstanding contribution to society in Ontario and around the world and is awarded to about 25 people each year for excellence and achievement in any field. Past recipients have contributed to education, the arts, community and public service, science and medicine, citizenship and multiculturalism, business, sports, and many other fields. Those who are invested into the Order of Ontario are considered an example of excellence to all Ontarians.

Individuals are nominated for the Order by members of the public. Then an Advisory Council recommends the most outstanding nominees to the Lieutenant Governor-in-Council.

The Order of Ontario medal is in the shape of the Ontario's floral emblem, the trillium. It includes Ontario's Shield of Arms and the Crown. The ribbon is red (the colour of the Ontario Ensign), white and green (the colours of the trillium), and gold. The member's name and year of investiture is engraved on the back of the medal.

The press release announcing Eva's selection said this about her:

Eva Olsson – a survivor of the concentration camps, Ms. Olsson, author and public speaker, travels across Ontario and North America to share her story. She inspires many with her dignity and faith and her contribution to education, community groups and associations.

The Order of Ontario certificate Eva received reads:

The Order of Ontario, established in 1986, has been created to honour service of the greatest distinction and of singular excellence in any field of endeavour benefiting society in Ontario and elsewhere. Eva Olsson, in recognition of outstanding contribution and Achievements, is hereby appointed to membership in the Order of Ontario together with the appropriate rights, Privileges and advantages.

On January 24, 2008 Eva, her son Jan and his wife Kim, her grandchildren Brenna, Rudy, and Alexandra, and her longtime friend Jackie Doran travelled to Toronto for the Order of Ontario investiture ceremony at Queen's Park, There she was presented with The Order of Ontario insignia, a certificate, and a lapel pin that identifies her as a recipient. This event was followed by a dinner at the Royal York Hotel.

Lieutenant-Governor David Onley, with the assistance of his Aide-de Camp

They asked me to speak on behalf of the recipients, so I spoke about the importance of doing good works. I used the example of planting positive seeds and nourishing them so they will grow. We may each choose to work in a different field, but the important thing is that we do make a choice and devote our energy to seeing that the seeds we plant grow and blossom.

This award couldn't have come at a better time, as it provided a bit of light after all the darkness of my recent journey. I was very excited when I heard the news, very proud to have been nominated for such an award. Like the [Honorary Doctor of Education] degree from Nipissing University, I didn't ask for it; it came to me.

Col. Sandy Cameron, presents Eva with the Order of Ontario.

On July 17, 2008, Eva received an invitation from the Council of the Royal College of Physicians and Surgeons of Canada, inviting her to accept Honorary Fellowship in the College.

Honorary Fellowship, under the terms of the Royal College Bylaws, is bestowed upon distinguished physicians, surgeons or other laypersons as the Council, the College's governing body, may deem fit. Your outstanding contributions through speaking on issues of compassion, humanity and healing were very clearly seen by our Council to be deserving of this award. Honorary Fellowship entitles you to use the designation FRCSPC.

The award ceremony is to take place in conjunction with the

Royal College's Annual Conference on Friday, September 26, 2008, in Ottawa, Ontario.

When people ask me how long I intend to do this important work, I remind them that bullying and genocide are still happening in many parts of the world. Unfortunately, because these problems—caused by hate and intolerance—will always be with us, I'm going to keep speaking as long as I can.

Then I can honestly say to the millions of people whose voices were so cruelly silenced by the Nazis, "You have not been forgotten."